A Simple Matter Of Belief

What is Belief?

Reverend Sharon M. White

WESTBOW
PRESS®
A DIVISION OF THOMAS NELSON
& ZONDERVAN

Copyright © 2018 Reverend Sharon M. White.

All rights reserved. No part of this book may be used or reproduced by any means, graphic, electronic, or mechanical, including photocopying, recording, taping or by any information storage retrieval system without the written permission of the author except in the case of brief quotations embodied in critical articles and reviews.

This book is a work of non-fiction. Unless otherwise noted, the author and the publisher make no explicit guarantees as to the accuracy of the information contained in this book and in some cases, names of people and places have been altered to protect their privacy.

WestBow Press books may be ordered through booksellers or by contacting:

WestBow Press
A Division of Thomas Nelson & Zondervan
1663 Liberty Drive
Bloomington, IN 47403
www.westbowpress.com
1 (866) 928-1240

Because of the dynamic nature of the Internet, any web addresses or links contained in this book may have changed since publication and may no longer be valid. The views expressed in this work are solely those of the author and do not necessarily reflect the views of the publisher, and the publisher hereby disclaims any responsibility for them.

Any people depicted in stock imagery provided by Getty Images are models, and such images are being used for illustrative purposes only.
Certain stock imagery © Getty Images.

ISBN: 978-1-9736-3633-5 (sc)
ISBN: 978-1-9736-3632-8 (e)

Library of Congress Control Number: 2018909712

Print information available on the last page.

WestBow Press rev. date: 8/22/2018

Scripture taken from the King James Version of the Bible.

Scripture taken from the New King James Version®. Copyright © 1982 by Thomas Nelson. Used by permission. All rights reserved.

Scripture quotations marked (NIV) are taken from the Holy Bible, New International Version®, NIV®. Copyright © 1973, 1978, 1984, 2011 by Biblica, Inc.™ Used by permission of Zondervan. All rights reserved worldwide. www.zondervan.com The "NIV" and "New International Version" are trademarks registered in the United States Patent and Trademark Office by Biblica, Inc.™

Scripture quotations marked (NLT) are taken from the Holy Bible, New Living Translation, copyright ©1996, 2004, 2015 by Tyndale House Foundation. Used by permission of Tyndale House Publishers, Inc., Carol Stream, Illinois 60188. All rights reserved.

Scripture quotations marked (TLB) are taken from The Living Bible copyright © 1971. Used by permission of Tyndale House Publishers, Inc., Carol Stream, Illinois 60188. All rights reserved.

The Holy Bible, English Standard Version® (ESV®). Copyright © 2001 by Crossway, a publishing ministry of Good News Publishers. All rights reserved. ESV Text Edition: 2016

Scripture quotations marked (GNT) are from the Good News Translation in Today's English Version- Second Edition Copyright © 1992 by American Bible Society. Used by Permission.

Scriptures and additional materials quoted are from the Good News Bible © 1994 published by the Bible Societies/HarperCollins Publishers Ltd UK, Good News Bible© American Bible Society 1966, 1971, 1976, 1992. Used with permission.

Scripture is taken from GOD'S WORD®, © 1995 God's Word to the Nations. Used by permission of Baker Publishing Group.

Scripture quotations marked (LEB) are from the Lexham English Bible. Copyright 2012 Logos Bible Software. Lexham is a registered trademark of Logos Bible Software.

Scripture taken from the American Standard Version of the Bible.

The Holy Bible: International Standard Version. Release 2.0, Build 2015.02.09. Copyright © 1995-2014 by ISV Foundation. ALL RIGHTS RESERVED INTERNATIONALLY. Used by permission of Davidson Press, LLC.

Scripture taken from the Easy-to-Read Version of the Bible. Copyright © 2006 by Bible League international.

Scripture taken from the World English Bible.

Scripture taken from The Bible in Basic English.

Scripture taken from the Revised Version of the Bible.

Scripture taken from the Literal Translation of the Holy Bible. Copyright © 1976 - 2000 By Jay P. Green, Sr. Used by permission of the copyright holder. Courtesy of Sovereign Grace Publishers and Christian Literature World

Dedication

This book is dedicated to everyone that is seeking Truth; to allow a spiritual awakening, through a relationship with Jesus Christ to find God within.

Acknowledgment

Writing this book has been a journey, I am very grateful for all the people who have encouraged me to keep writing. A special thanks goes to:

The Holy Spirit, for being my guide and councilor in life;

My husband Neil, for his love and support;

A very special friend Katheryn Williams, who has walked with me on this journey;

I also thank my Dad, who transitioned from this life at the age of eighty, for inspiring me to take each day and in-brace it.

Contents

Preface xiii
Introduction xv

1. What Is Belief? 1
2. A Carnal Mind 9
3. Wisdom 15
4. The Great I am 27
5. The Emphasis of I am 31
6. I am the Way and the Truth and the Life 35
7. The Bread of Life 45
8. I am the Door of My Sheep 51
9. I am the Good Shepherd 55
10. I am the True Vine 59
11. I am the Resurrection and the Life 63
12. I Am the Light of the World 75

Conclusion 95
Bibliography 101
About the Author 103
About the Book 105

Preface

When I was young I was influenced by two very different beliefs, the Church I went to with my Mother told me how bad I was. Then I would go to another church with my dad and great aunt, there they would tell me how special I am and how much God love me.

When I was older I started to seek out other churches, I found that the dialogue was just as bewildering. Most of the time I felt guilt and had very low self-worth while trying to love God, it was a struggle. So, I walked away from the organized church way of life.

I came to a point in my life where I said to God "If you are real and truly do exist, you will show me the truth." Time went by and I relocated to another city. On my way to work one morning as clear as day I heard this voice, it said "Go to that church"

Who said that? What church? I had been driving the same route for months and never saw a church. That night I went to look for this church, sure enough there it was; the next Sunday I planned to go. It was over ten years since I had been in a church

That Sunday morning I walked through the doors of that church, a very astonishing women greeted me; she stood about four feet tall and look to be three hundred years old. She said "glad you chose to come, follow Me.", she walked down the aisle and sat me at the front of the church.

After the service the pastor asked if there was first time visitors, a few people put up their hand, so I did as well. He asked each of us to introduce ourselves when I told him my name he said "God told me you would be coming".

What I had said to God a few years earlier, He showed me: He is real and truly dose exist and it was within the walls of that church I started on my journey of knowing and my believing in Jesus.

If you are wondering about the women that greeted me at the door: the pastor did not know who I was asking about, no one else knew that person either. None the less, her words have stayed with me all of these years "glad you choose to come, follow me."

I am now launching into a writing ministry, to share with you the Truth. My hope is that you will join me on this wonderful journey.

Introduction

Beliefs are defined as inward convictions; a feeling of certainty about what something meaningful. They are embedded deeply within us. A belief is both mental and emotional. It is established in the mind and in the heart. Do you know that our beliefs will dictate our actions? If we believe in a cause, we support it. When we believe in others, we assistance and strengthen them. Beliefs drive us! Beliefs are at the root of all intents and all actions. Belief can empower us and put limits on us.

The word belief comes from two words. Be and life, "Be" comes from being, which is a state of existence. To be, is to live. The second part of the word "Life" comes from the Indo-European word, "leubh" which means – love. So when you put those concepts together, it changes the entire idea of the word belief. Belief means: to be in love with. In Matthew, Jesus was asked a question by a lawyer, "which is the great commandment in the law"? Jesus answered in Matthew:

Jesus said to him, 'YOU SHALL LOVE THE LORD YOUR GOD WITH ALL YOUR HEART, WITH ALL YOUR SOUL, AND WITH ALL YOUR MIND.' This is the first and great commandment. And the second is like it: 'YOU SHALL LOVE YOUR NEIGHBOR AS YOURSELF.' Matthew 22:37-39 (NKJV).

What Jesus is really saying to them and to us we must believe our God Jesus makes this very clear "Truly, truly, I say to you, He who hears My Word and believes on Him who sent Me has everlasting life and shall not come into condemnation, but has passed from death to life." John 5:24 (NKJV).

This is why when Paul wrote to the Romans: "If you confess with your mouth that Jesus is Lord and believe in your heart that God raised Him from the dead, you will be saved. For it is by believing in your heart that you are made right with God, and it is by confessing with your mouth that you are saved." Romans 10:9-10 (NLT).

Paul wrote this because Jesus said: "Offspring of vipers! How can you, being evil, speak good things? For out of the **abundance of the heart the mouth speaks**. A good man out of the good treasure of the heart brings out good things; and an evil man out of the evil treasure brings out evil things." Matthew 12:34-35 (NKJV).

Belief as very little to do with information or whether we know or understand all the facts; all we really need is to know is just how much God truly loves His Son and us. It takes actual knowledge, which is a realistic process and changes it to love, which is a function of the heart. A true belief is something that echoes both in heart and mind.

Think about it this way: We just need to start with one fact, God love us. "For God loved the world so much that he gave his only Son, so that everyone who believes in him may not die but have eternal life. "John 3:16 (GNB).

When we can truly believe in that statement, we are really saying: "We love Him"

Let me give you an illustration. If we love someone, we will act on that love by showing respect, caring for their wellbeing, helping when we can. That is what God did and does for us. God acted when man fell in the Garden of Eden. God initiated the plan to restore mankind into a relationship with the Father through Jesus.

"The Lord is not slow to fulfill his promise as some count slowness, but is patient toward you, not wishing that any should perish, but that all should reach repentance." 2 Peter 3:9 (ESV).

You may be saying this is faith; Lets looks at a Faith-based belief. Some will say that it is a system of mental concepts that is absence of evidence. I am not saying this to criticize, rather to define an important difference. In short, a faith-based belief system is unmistakably based on the lack of evidence impossible to collect. This is not the case when it comes to God and Jesus:

"They know the truth about God because He has made it obvious to them. For ever since the world was created, people have seen the earth and sky. Through everything God made, they can clearly see His invisible qualities—His eternal power and divine nature. So they have no excuse for not knowing God." Romans 1:19-20 (NLT).

This book will to help us understand the evidence as to how God and Jesus acted out for us, and help us to see all the data from a different aspect, being God's aspect!

1

What Is Belief?

What is Belief?

What is belief? It is the psychological state in which an individual holds an idea or assumption to be true. What is truth? Truth most often means *in accord with fact* or *reality to an original or a standard ideal*.

When I think about the meaning of these words Truth and Belief, I ask myself, "what I once knew to be true can no longer be truth, based on the fact or reality of the ideal". Let's look at two truths (beliefs) that are no longer true.

I was told the story that Columbus set out to prove that the world was round not flat, by sailing west. This was a historical fact for many of us; the truth is that the ancient Greeks knew the earth was not flat. Today that historical reference is no longer truth, as it was debunked by the late nineteenth century.

Did you know that more than two thousand years, before Columbus, people knew that the earth was round? They knew this just by looking around them. They may have asked questions about the world but, I would reason, not that it was flat. People saw certain stars in the night sky from one location, and this is how they charted maps, as these same stars were not seen from another location. Even in the natural day-to-day life of watching a ship sail away, they would see that the bottom of a ship disappeared first over the horizon before the top. The questions that may have been asked about the world moved the mind of one man:

Eratosthenes of Cyrene (Ancient Greece) lived from 276 BCE to

195 BCE. He was a Greek mathematician, geographer, poet, music theorist, and last but not least, an astronomer. He was the first person to use the word *geography*, and he invented the discipline of geography as we understand it today. He invented the system of latitude and longitude. In 255 BCE, he also invented the armillary sphere on the circular motions of the celestial bodies. He was credited for having calculated the earth's circumference around 240 BCE, using knowledge of the angle of the elevation of the sun at noon on the summer solstice in Alexandria and on Elephantine Island.

The belief of a flat earth was actually debunked in 1991 by Jeffrey Burton Russell (born 1934) is a well published American historian and religious studies scholar. Jeffrey Burton Russell says the flat-earth error flourished most between 1870 and 1920; even today, the flat-earth belief is still common. When asked who discovered that the world was actually round, most people will answer "Columbus". I am sometimes shocked by comments I get from sceptics that said the Bible, talked about a flat-earth.

A man named Alfred Wegener (1880–1930) was an accomplished German natural scientist in the fields of meteorology, astronomy, and geology. He came up with what was called the Pangaea theory in 1912, which was treated with much skepticism when the information was presented. But since then, much evidence has supported this theory. His theory of Pangaea was that many years ago, all the continents were joined together in one enormous land mass, known as Pangaea. This name comes from an Ancient Greek word meaning "Earth." For some unknown reason, the land mass divided and created the continents we have today. He wrote a book about this called *The Origin of Continents and Oceans.* His theory went on to say that the continents will continue to drift until they meet again in a different configuration.

I have read this same information in the Bible. "Then God said, "Let the waters beneath the sky flow together into one place, so dry ground may appear." And that is what happened. God called the dry ground "land" and the waters "seas." And God saw that it was good." Genesis 1:9-10 (NLT).

Since the beginning of history, humans have dreamed of the ability to soar on the wind with wings and to have the freedom of birds, but history and folklore is full of rebukes against man flying. Icarus of Greek mythology fashioned wings of wax and feathers and then flew too close to the sun. The wax melted, and the feathers came loose, and Icarus plunged to his death in the sea. He had dared to go beyond his place in life and was properly smitten for his audacity.

Leonardo da Vinci was fascinated by the phenomenon of flight, producing many studies of the flight of birds, including his *Codex on the Flight of Birds* (circa 1505), as well as plans for several flying machines, including a light hang glider and a machine resembling a helicopter.

Around 294 years later came Sir George Cayley, an English engineer and one of the most important people in the history of aeronautics. Many consider him the first true scientific aerial investigator and the first person to understand the underlying principles and forces of flight. In 1799, he set forth the concept of the modern airplane as a fixed-wing flying machine, with separate systems for lift, propulsion, and control. He is sometimes referred to as the father of aerodynamics. As the designer of the first successful glider to carry a human being aloft, he discovered and identified the four aerodynamic forces of flight—weight, lift, drag, and thrust—which act on any modern airplane design today.

In 1883, Octave Chanute became interested in aviation when he retired from his railroad career. He decided to devote his leisure time to furthering the new science of aviation. Applying his engineering background, Chanute collected all available data from flight experimenters around the world. He published his findings in a series of articles in *The Railroad and Engineering Journal* from 1891 to 1893.

In 1901, we get to the Wright brothers. The brothers had nearly given up in defeat. They had based their wing designs on the work of predecessors, pioneers who were widely respected within the scientific community. Just like those predecessors, the Wright brothers discovered that all of it was in error. One day, after unsuccessful gliding experiments. Wilbur Wright, in hopelessness, made this statement: **"Not within a thousand years will man ever fly."** This was the truth. After the brothers got the new information they were airborne. One hundred and seventeen years later, millions of people fly all over the world, daily!

We as people, put our beliefs into some strange things. Look at the event that took place on October 30 when a CBS radio station broadcast an adaptation of H. G. Wells' novel *The War of the Worlds*. Many listeners panicked, believing that the nation had been invaded by Martians. Some people loaded blankets and supplies in their cars.

By the time the night was over, however, almost all of these people had learned that the news broadcast was entirely fictitious. It was simply the weekly broadcast of Orson Welles and the Mercury Theater. That week, in honor of Halloween, they had decided to stage a highly dramatized and updated version of the H. G. Wells story. In the days following the broadcast, there was still widespread outrage and panic by certain listeners who had believed the events described in the program were real. They believed this because, they heard it on the radio.

Are we any better today? Let me ask you: what did you believed about Y2K and what about the Mayan calendar saying the world will end on December 21, 2012. Did you believe the Mayans? The Bible unmistakably tells us that no one knows the date or time of Jesus return, not even the angles or even Jesus himself which he tells us in Matthew 24:36 (LITV)-"But as to that day and that hour, no one knows, neither the angels of Heaven, except My Father only." Since the Bible tells us we won't know what day Jesus is returning we cannot say it was that day. But, what is up with that date? In Maya calendric system, it's not the end of a thousand years. It's the end of Baktun 13. The Maya calendar was based on multiple cycles of time, and the Baktun was one of them. A Baktun is 144,000.

Just for fun, let's see what you know. The following phrases are used in our day-to-day lives. If you know the phrase is from the Bible, place a small mark by it. Don't use your Bible to check; just use your memory:

- No cross, no crown
- Money is the root of all evil
- Bread is the staff of life
- Let your conscience be your guide
- Know thyself
- To err is human, to forgive is divine
- God helps those who help themselves
- God's glory is His goodness
- Familiarity breeds contempt

So how many of these phrases are from the Bible?

The answer:

None

2

A Carnal Mind

A Carnal Mind

How much of what we believe is really the truth? Sometimes, our beliefs are imbalanced. In general, in whatever we face today, we base our beliefs and direct our lives on the information we have on hand at the moment. When it comes to making a decision, we look at our past successes or our unsuccessful attempts at life. This is a human weakness. This is what Paul is talking about in Romans—a carnal mind.

Paul writes Romans 8:5-8 (LEB): "For those who are living according to the flesh are intent on the things of the flesh, but those who are living according to the Spirit are intent on the things of the Spirit. For the mindset of the flesh is death, but the mindset of the Spirit is life and peace, because the mindset of the flesh is enmity toward God, for it is not subjected to the law of God, for it is not able to do so, and those who are in the flesh are not able to please God."

Let us look at this word *carnal*. The word *carnal* is translated from the Greek word *"sarkikos"*, which literally means "fleshly". A carnal mind is how we reason information from our five senses. We believed the world was flat because the teacher said so. The Wright brothers believed man would not fly because the test flight had failed. The people listening to the *War of the Worlds* broadcast trusted and believed in the information they got from the radio. There was no difference with us as 1999 came to an end. On January 1, 2000, life as we knew it would be changed forever. On that day the computers on which we all depended would crash. That was the day that all of our comforts of daily life would collapse, and we would be shaken to live without electricity power, water, and heat. The Y2K scare is what it was called. The panic was that all of our computer systems, everywhere, would terminate at midnight on December 31, 1999. The new millennium appears to have dawned without any ruckus, as we watched and waited for January 1, 2000; digital peace was here to stay with all our comforts of daily life.

This is what it means to be carnally minded. Carnally minded is to be facts minded, all five sense rule our emotions; we are driven environmental circumstances. The carnal mind always is focused on the facts and problems, not on the word of God. The simple truth of it is, to be carnally minded means: you have a mindset that is contrary to God and His Word.

This is why Paul tells us to be spiritually minded, which means to have God's view and opinion. That is what Paul is talking about when he said, "For to be carnally minded is death; but to be spiritually minded is life and peace". Romans 8:6 (KJV).

The thoughts of our minds, become what we believe, and what we believe—becomes our opinions. We are, then, the sum total of what we believe. Paul also tells us: "For those who live according to the flesh set their minds on the things of the flesh, but those who live according to the Spirit, the things of the Spirit" Romans 8:5 (NKJV). So if we believe according to God's beliefs, then there is no limitation on God's grace in our lives.

As believers, can we still be carnal minded? The answer to this question is: "And I, brethren, could not speak unto you as unto spiritual, but as unto carnal, as unto babes in Christ. I fed you with milk, not with meat; for ye were not yet able to bear it: nay, not even now are ye able; for ye are yet carnal: for whereas there is among you jealousy and strife, are ye not carnal, and do ye not walk after the manner of men?" 1 Corinthians 3:1-3 (ASV).

The apostle Paul addresses the readers as "brethren", a term he uses almost exclusively to refer to other believers. Paul goes on to describe them as "carnal". Therefore, we can conclude that believers can be carnal. We must understand, however, that while a believer can be carnal, a true believer will not remain carnal. After all, we are told in "Do not be conformed to this world, but continually be transformed by the renewing of your minds so that you may be able to determine what God's will is—what is proper, pleasing, and perfect." Romans 12:2 (ISV).

Paul is telling us that we need to change the way we think. We need to look to the present each and every moment. When we understand the word of God, we know that *HE* cares for us. The historical accounts in the Bible tell us that fact. Think of Daniel when he was throw in with the lions, he curled up with one and had a good night sleep. How often do we lay in bed and worry about the next day or week? All we have done is watch the minutes tick by and lost a good night's sleep.

The mind is strange. It will talk us into doing things we know are not right, like eating that big bowl of double-chocolate ice cream before bed, or it will talk us out of following our dreams by recalling negative past experiences. Our self-chatter will say, "Remember when you did this or that?"

Here are a few points on how the mind works:

- The mind does not want to lose control
- "I am always right" (ego)
- The mind will define us by what the world said we are
- The mind will fight change

Paul tells us: "This means that anyone who belongs to Christ has become a new person. The old life is gone; a new life has begun!" 2 Corinthians 5:17 (NLT).

We must sometimes eliminate our five senses, replacing them with encouraging acknowledgment from the Word of God. Spiritually minded means, with the Word of God. We need to establish a persona of realizing every situation we confront that is fear-provoking stacked against us it can cause us to lose hold of your thinking. When we allow ourselves to be Spiritually minded we easily evolve form stress into love, joy, peace, patience, kindness, goodness, gentleness, faithfulness and self-control of the Spirit because the Holy Spirit is the strength that produces these spiritual fruits. A spiritual mindset is the mind of Christ in driving, we no longer feel helpless on sheer human understanding and interpretation.

Even in the church, we have relied on others understanding and interpretation driven from their five senses relating to their life experiences, rather than living out of the spirit. When we do this it closes off the Holy Spirit from speaking to us through our spirit and we ignore a revelation of knowledge and discernment by our spirit through our spiritual senses.

In Paul's letter to the Corinthians he writes to them, "For the weapons of our warfare are not merely human, but powerful to God for the tearing down of fortresses, tearing down arguments and all pride that is raised up against the knowledge of God, and taking every thought captive to the obedience of Christ." 2 Corinthians 10:4-5 (LEB).

There are only two ways a mind works one is carnally minded, two is spiritually minded; there is no "in between". We either have the mindset of the natural world and we are facts only focused or we give place to the mindset of the spirit which is based on the truth of God's Word. This is what Paul is telling us it should be a part of our thinking process every day.

We must take every thought captive, check every thought to see if it is fact based, circumstantial evidence based on are five senses or if it is of the truth of God's Word.

John writes a letter to his friend Gaius, in his greeting, John gives us words of wisdom when he wrote: "Dear friend, I pray you may prosper concerning everything and be healthy, just as your soul prospers." 3 John 1:2 (LEB)

Our spirit man and soul can only prosper when it is centered on the truth of God's Word, rather than circumstantial evidence or the facts. Carnally minded or spiritually minded, which will you choose? Each day we have to make the choice in any given situation.

3

Wisdom

Wisdom

With wisdom, we reject negative thoughts. Can you define wisdom? Don't run for your dictionary. Even when we look up a word, sometimes the dictionary just doesn't quite fulfill our requirement. We read the definition and still do not have a complete understanding of the word; that's the way it is with wisdom. Solomon, the writer of Proverbs, tells us that Wisdom is the key to life.

"My father taught me, "Take my words to heart. Follow my commands, and you will live. Get wisdom; develop good judgment. Don't forget my words or turn away from them. Don't turn your back on wisdom, for she will protect you. Love her, and she will guard you. Getting wisdom is the wisest thing you can do! And whatever else you do, develop good judgment. If you prize wisdom, she will make you great. Embrace her, and she will honor you. She will place a lovely wreath on your head; she will present you with a beautiful crown." My child, listen to me and do as I say, and you will have a long, good life. I will teach you wisdom's ways and lead you in straight paths. When you walk, you won't be held back; when you run, you won't stumble. Take hold of my instructions; don't let them go. Guard them, for they are the key to life." Proverbs 4:4–13 (NLT).

Biblical wisdom should not merely be equated with knowledge or knowing something very well. Biblical wisdom is knowledge rightly applied. Biblical wisdom refers not only to what a person knows but to how a person lives.

Wisdom provides us with guidance:

"Who has wisdom and good sense among you? Let him make his works clear by a life of gentle wisdom. But if you have bitter envy in your heart and the desire to get the better of others, have no pride in this, talking falsely against what is true. This wisdom is not from heaven, but is of the earth and the flesh and the Evil One. For where envy is, and the desire to get the better of others, there is no order, but every sort of evil-doing. But the wisdom which is from heaven is first holy, then gentle, readily giving way in argument, full of peace and mercy and good works, not doubting, not seeming other than it is." James 3:13-17 (BBE).

Wisdom is not simply a grasp of information or knowledge but everyday applied application of God's truth to the routine events in our lives. Wisdom is mindfulness to every situation and person. Wisdom relates to developing a viewpoint on life. Wisdom is an approach of astonishment and meekness; it is a complete dependence upon God, not just when problems come into our lives but in every area of life. This is true is wisdom.

Let us take a look a historic event in the life of Solomon. Imagine for a moment if God came to you and said, "I will give you whatever you want." Take a moment and think about this question. God, who crafted the beauty of the heavens and everything on earth—yes, God Himself—is standing face-to-face with you. What would you ask for?

One man in the Bible, Solomon, had such an option. We find the following in 1 Kings; when God appeared to Solomon one night in a dream. God said to Solomon, "I will give you whatever you ask for"!

God is saying to Solomon, "Whatever you want." What an offer! Now, Solomon could have asked for anything—wealth, victory in battles, or even no more wars or great health. Just think about this offer he got. Let's look at what he asked for. "So give your servant an understanding mind to govern your people, so I can discern between good and evil. Otherwise, how will I be able to govern this great people of yours? The Lord was pleased that Solomon had asked for this" 1 Kings 3:9-10 (ESV).

God was pleased with his request. There are six hundred and fifty prayers in the Bible. Ten have been exhibited as great prayers of the Bible; Solomon's prayer is one of these. Why is this labeled as a great prayer, and why was God pleased?

Let us carefully examine what really took place here. First, let us try to understand what Solomon's concerns were. We have a few hints. Let's examine what Solomon said before his great prayer "And Solomon said: 'You have shown great mercy to Your servant David my father, because he walked before You in truth, in righteousness, and in uprightness of heart with You; You have continued this great kindness for him, and You have given him a son to sit on his throne, as it is this day". 1 Kings 3:6 (NKJV).

Solomon was associating himself with his father, King David. His father had ruled for forty years over Israel—seven and a half in Hebron and thirty-three in Jerusalem. King David's kingdom was firmly established and all of Israel's enemies were well restrained. King David died at the age of seventy and was buried in the City of David (Jerusalem).

If you recall the life story of David: God sent Samuel to anoint David when David was a young boy. We see this 1 Samuel. "And Samuel said to Jesse, 'Are all the young men here?' Then he said, 'There remains yet the youngest, and there he is, keeping the sheep.' And Samuel said to Jesse, 'Send and bring him. For we will not sit down till he comes here.' So he sent and brought him in. Now he was ruddy, with bright eyes, and good-looking. And the Lord said, 'Arise, anoint him; for this is the one!' Then Samuel took the horn of oil and anointed him in the midst of his brothers; and the Spirit of the Lord." 1 Samuel 16:1113 (NKJV).

When we know the historical events of David's life, we can start understand how his son, Solomon may have felt. After all, we are told that David was a man after God's own heart. "And when He had removed him, He raised up for them David as king, to whom also He gave testimony and said, 'I have found David the son of Jesse, a man after My own heart, who will do all My will' ". Acts 13:22 (NKJV).

The first thing we can say is that Solomon may have felt very overwhelmed. He may have wondered, "Is God just being nice to me because He loves my father so much?" Or he may have thought, "Do I even have the right to rule a kingdom?" King David was a big act to follow. How often does life make us feel this way? Can we relate to how Solomon was feeling, where we have stepped into someone else's shoes to do a job or have been given a responsibility?

Now let's look at another hint. "Now, O Lord my God, You have made Your servant king instead of my father David, but I am a little child; I do not know how to go out or come in". 1 Kings 3:7 (NKJV).

Solomon is revealing that he feels like a child. Let us not interpret this to say he was a child. We know this was just an exaggeration, based primarily on his feelings. He was most likely had doubt, was he up to the role of king and allot of depressing viewpoint.

We are not told the date when Solomon was born, but by looking closely at what is written, we can estimate how old he was. Solomon was born well after David became king, David conquered the Jebusite stronghold of Jerusalem, and David made it the capital. God had made a covenant with David, promising to establish the house of David: "Your throne shall be established forever." 2 Samuel 7:16 (LEB). David wins victories over the Philistines, and the Moabites and Hadadezer of Zobah paid tribute for many years, when by chance, he met Bathsheba.

"It happened in the spring of the year, at the time when kings go out to battle, that David sent Joab and his servants with him, and all Israel; and they destroyed the people of Ammon and besieged Rabbah. But David remained at Jerusalem. Then it happened one evening that David arose from his bed and walked on the roof of the king's house. And from the roof he saw a woman bathing, and the woman was very beautiful to behold. So David sent and inquired about the woman. And someone said, "Is this not Bathsheba, the daughter of Eliam, the wife of Uriah the Hittite?" 2 Samuel 11:1–3 (NKJV).

Several more years followed. There was the first pregnancy and the death of the first child and then the second pregnancy. It is safe to estimate that David may have been king for about ten years, which means that Solomon was in his early to mid-twenties when he became king. Remember, too, that Solomon got married, we are told this in 1 Kings 3:1(LEB) when Solomon made a treaty with king of Egypt, and married his daughter. This information also suggests that he was in his mid-twenties. We can see now that what Solomon really was saying is, "I don't have what it takes to be a king." This really is a humble confession he makes to God. He does not feel that he has the confidence or the experience to rule.

Last but not least, we have the third hint provided in 1 Kings 3:8 (NKJV)—"And your servant is in the midst of Your people whom You have chosen, a great people, too numerous to be numbered or counted". Solomon may have been thinking, these people are God's chosen people! Who am I to think I can rule them? He was king over people too many to count. I think it is safe to say that Solomon may have thought it was laughable and felt greatly overwhelmed.

When our day-to-day lives become overwhelming, and we go to bed with much of the day's events on our minds, we may be weighed down with doubt and worry. It is not a leap to think that when Solomon went to bed at night, all these questions were weighing heavily on his mind and most likely had been profoundly in his thoughts since he became king.

Solomon encountered God in a dream, and God said to Solomon, "What can I give you?" Why did the Lord give Solomon complete freedom to request anything of Him?

Before we can consider Solomon's prayer, we need to know two important facts. The writer of 1 Kings makes this statement: "And Solomon loved the Lord" and in 2 Samuel 12:24 (NKJV) the announcement of Solomon's birth is followed by this statement: "The Lord loved him." So we see that from these two statement that God loved Solomon even before he was born. John tell us the reader of his day and us in 1 John 4:19 (KJV)—"We love Him because He first loved us." God loved Solomon, just as He loves us today.

We know that Solomon's prayer is an appeal in a loving relationship with the God. We know that Solomon did not think of God as being unfriendly or somewhere far off. Solomon did not see God as a cosmic slot machine that responded unconsciously to the requests from His creation. Solomon knew the God of the universe in a personal, loving, and big-hearted fashion. Solomon had a loving relationship with God, and God had a loving relationship with Solomon.

A loving relationship—Solomon and God were in love. Love is not a feeling, it is the reality of oneness. That is what God wants with us. God loves us just the way we are, we don't need to make an impression on God. By being yourself in this relationship with God will inspire you to mature and with that understanding, and give you the freedom to follow your dreams. God always has our back, He is for us!

When we spend time getting to know God, we have assurance that God is with us: the reality of oneness. When we do not have a relationship, we are like those described by Isaiah 59:2 (ESV) — "Your iniquities have made a separation between you and your God, and your sins have hidden His face from you, so that He does not hear [you]."

Now that we have some insight into this prayer, we can see that there are those who think of God as a slot machine—pull the handle and hope for three cherries. This is praying in vain. Then there are those who seek a loving relationship with Him. This is the determining factor you see David was inspired by God's omniscience God is all-knowing and all-wise and David's son learned this from David. We sometimes forget about God, but God never forgets about us. He is always available for us if we "seek Him with all your heart" as we are told in Deuteronomy "But from there you will seek the LORD your God, and you will find Him if you seek Him with all your heart and with all your soul." Deuteronomy

4:29 (NKJV). This is the determining factor whether we are seeking God and our Lord in a loving relationship.

Upon the death of his father King David, Solomon became very powerful and wealthy. He obtained his status on the throne as a young man. A young man with all that power and wealth could have look down on others and walked about with exalted puffed-up chest, saying, "My father is dead, and I am now the almighty king of Israel!" Solomon did not do that. He humbled himself and humbly professed to the Lord, "I am but a child; I do not know how to go out or to come in" 1 Kings 3:7 (NKJV).

We see Solomon as a prevailing man. After all, he was a king to most of the known world at that time. However, Solomon knew God, in comparison to God, with whom he was conferring, Solomon was very weak.

Why do we wait until life and its problems overtake us, and then we run to God, pull the handle, and hope three cherries show up? We do this, believing that God is somehow duty-bound to give us whatever we ask for. This often is our approach to prayer! Why is it so challenging for us to go to God and confess that we come to Him from a position of weakness? Undoubtedly, we can learn from Solomon's prayer that before we pray, we need to seek God with genuine thankfulness and praise and with a humble attitude. Solomon went to God with an honorable petition.

What is God's perspective on Solomon's prayer? This could be a risky thing to determine. I do not know the mind of God, nor do I desire to put words in His mouth. However, from the study of His words and seeking Him, I feel secure in telling you this.

There are 836 references to the heart in the Bible. This is a really good clue that God is a "heart" God. Another clue is what Jesus himself said " You offspring of snakes, how are you, being evil, able to say good things? Because out of the heart's store come the words of the mouth. Matthew 12:34 (BBE).

God knew Solomon's heart. He saw this man, His child, who was fearful and anxious. God knew that Solomon wanted so desperately to be a good ruler like his father David. As well, he knew deep in his heart that without God, he would be unable to lead God's chosen people. From this example we see that we just have to be straightforward foremost with ourselves and then with God.

After Solomon is done his prayer we see that God's is pleased "The Lord was pleased that Solomon had asked for wisdom."1 Kings 3:10 (NLT). God made him greater than his father, King David.

"So God replied, "Because you have asked for wisdom in governing My people with justice and have not asked for a long life or wealth or the death of your enemies— I will give you what you asked for! I will give you a wise and understanding heart such as no one else has had or ever will have! And I will also give you what you did not ask for—riches and fame! No other king in all the world will be compared to you for the rest of your life!" 1 Kings 3:11-13 (NLT)

I have asked the question, "If God came to you and said I will give you whatever you want, what would you ask for?" That is what God said to Solomon. It seemed that God was handing over to Solomon a blank check with no conditions, but then, God said: "And if you follow Me and obey My decrees and My commands as your father, David, did, I will give you a long life." Kings 3:14 (NLT). It appears that God placed conditions on Solomon's request.

To understand this fully, we have to look at verse 14. Here, the Lord makes a condition to Solomon by saying, "If you walk in My ways, keeping My statutes and commandments, as your father David walked, then I will prolong your days."

When we read this account, it looks like God went from unconditional to conditional. Why the switch? Have you ever thought about this? Does this tell us that the promises of God have conditions or are to be earned? No, that is not what God is saying here. Let's look closely at the nature of the condition. God is asking, not demanding or putting a condition on anything. He is simply telling us, "Walk in My ways." God is saying, "Keep My statutes."

This is the application of wisdom; this is knowledge rightly applied. The Lord is simply asking Solomon to be a good steward.

In re-examining this historical account, we now have a better understanding of God. You might ask, "What does this have to do with me today?" This was in the Old Testament, and this is true. God made an oath:

"God also bound Himself with an oath, so that those who received the promise could be perfectly sure that He would never change His mind. So God has given both His promise and His oath. These two things are unchangeable because it is impossible for God to lie." Hebrews 6:17-18 (NLT).

This world can be complex these days, sometimes we may wonder if God is even concerned. Solomon's account and other historical accounts in the Bible tell us that God never leaves us, even in the midst of confusion He is with us. When we understand that God is for us, our viewpoint is modify. We no longer become overwhelmed by our difficulties, we know that God has our back and He is blessing us.

God took an oath and made a promise. He fulfilled that promise though Jesus. Jesus came to earth because God loves us. Jesus loves God, so He came to provide us with the truth. Jesus came into a world of false beliefs.

Jesus Himself makes this statement: "All that the Father gives to Me shall come to Me, and the one coming to Me I will in no way cast out. For I have come down out of Heaven, not that I should do My will, but the will of Him who sent Me. And this is the will of the Father sending Me, that of all that He has given Me, I shall not lose any of it, but shall raise it up in the last day. And this is the will of the One sending Me, that everyone seeing the Son and believing into Him should have everlasting life; and I will raise him up at the last day." John 6:37-40 (LITV).

God's love impelled Jesus to come to earth and become a man to accomplish what only He Himself could do. Jesus liberated mankind. That means you and I are freed from bondage and fear. God gave the law, but the law was only a shadow, the law could not reconcile us to God. Only His Son, Jesus could restore what was lost. That is why Jesus is **<u>LORD.</u>** Jesus made the Way to God.

What is faith? Most people, think that faith and belief are the same thing. However, there are differences. Let's look at these two words to give us a better understanding. First what does belief mean? Dictionaries clarify, it as a state of mind that a person thinks something to be true with the current information they have at the moment. For example some believe that a big breakfast is best while others believe that a big lunch is best.

Faith on the other hand comes from our belief, we cannot have faith unless we first have a belief. The information we have today tells us that we will be healthy if we get a good night's sleep, eat wholesome foods and exercise. We believe this information to be true, so we try every day to do this. Faith is more of an action we choose.

The writer if Hebrew tells us—"Now faith is assurance of things hoped for, proof of things not seen." Hebrews 11:1 (WEB). So as you see, when we believe something to be true we take action with the confidence; we eat well, get eight hours of sleep every night and exercise to have good health.

Now that we understand the difference between the two, we have a better understanding as why Salmon asked for wisdom. Knowing the truth and being more strongly convinced of the truth we become and the more confident we'll grow in our faith then with confidence it allows us to take action when we take action we exercise our faith and miraculous things just happen.

It is just that simple. Jesus said it this "So Jesus answered and said to them, "Jesus answered them, "Most certainly I tell you, if you have faith, and don't doubt, you will not only do what was done to the fig tree, but even if you told this mountain, 'Be taken up and cast into the sea,' it would be done. All things, whatever you ask in prayer, believing, you will receive." Matthew 21:21-22 (WEB).

What is the meaning of faith? ***It's in the Bible***, "What is faith? It is the confident assurance that something we want is going to happen. It is the certainty that what we hope for is waiting for us, even though we cannot see it up ahead." Hebrews 11:1 (TLB).

Jesus is the source of faith. "So faith comes by hearing, and hearing by the word of God." Romans 10:17 (WEB).

Real faith is believing in what Christ has done for us. *It's in the Bible*, "So now, since we have been made right in God's sight by faith in his promises, we can have real peace with Him because of what Jesus Christ our Lord has done for us." Romans 5:1 (TLB).

Faith is trusting God in everything. *It's in the Bible*, "And those whose faith has made them good in God's sight must live by faith, trusting Him in everything. Otherwise, if they shrink back, God will have no pleasure in them." Hebrews 10:38 (TLB).

Weak faith can become strong faith with God's help. *It's in the Bible*, "The father instantly replied, 'I do have faith; oh, help me to have more!' " Mark 9:24 (TLB).

Our faith has to be grounded in the truth of God's Word. The beginning is in knowing who Jesus truly is. The truth gives us the capability to believe, and when we believe, we have faith. Where do we find the truth of Jesus? In His "I AM" statements.

4

The Great I am

The Great I am

Let's get to know who God really is by taking a journey, a deeper look at what we know and what we believe. Thought out the time Jesus was here on earth with us He made some insightful statements this is one of them Jesus said to them, "Most certainly, I tell you, before Abraham came into existence, I AM." John 8:58 (WEB).

Jesus is not saying that He lived before Abraham's what He is saying is that Abraham was just born into being, but Jesus existed from the very being, The people of the time understood what Jesus had said and believed it to be a lie they took up stones to kill Him, Jesus was with God and is impossible to tell apart God.

Jesus also tells us "If you had known Me, you would have known My Father also; and from now on you know Him and have seen Him" John 14:7 (NKJV). Jesus is saying, "If you know Me then you know the Father." This is where our journey begins, with a fundamental question: What do we know and believe about Jesus Christ? Since Jesus' earthly ministry began, people have been asking, "Who is this Jesus?"

It started many years ago when Jesus rode into Jerusalem on the back of a donkey, as he had come into Jerusalem, all the city was stirred up, saying, "Who is this?" Matthew 21:10 (WEB).

Have you ever asked yourself that question, "Who is Jesus?" This question still needs to be asked today. If we are to experience the Christ of the Bible, then we must have insight to what to believe.

After all, Jesus said Jesus said to him, "I am the way, the truth, and the life. No one comes to the Father, except through me. John 14:6 (WEB).

As we begin our journey through the great statements of Jesus, my hope is that you will come to know Jesus in an exceeding new way. He states that he is "the Resurrection," "the Light of the World," "the Door," and "the Good Shepherd." But in the text before us, the one I love the most is where Jesus simply identifies Himself as "I AM".

Have you ever given these two words any thought: "I AM"? We first see this in the Bible in Exodus God had appeared to Moses in a burning bush that wouldn't burn up. God told Moses that he was the man to lead the Israelites out of their bondage in Egypt. When Moses requested that God give him a name to tell the Israelites who had sent him, we learn: "And God said to Moses, "I AM THAT I AM". And He said, so you shall say to the sons of Israel, I AM has sent me to you." Exodus 3:14 (NKJV) to Moses, you. God went on to say, "This is my name forever, the name by which I AM to be remembered from generation to generation." Exodus 3:15 (NKJV).

Many generations have come and gone on this earth since God said this and today we are yet another generation, and God is still God, and Jesus is still Jesus. The writer of Hebrews tells us, that they are the same yesterday and forever.

God is still madly in love with us, no matter what we do. The question is, do we really believe it? It is a matter of belief. The great I AM loves you!!! Do you believe this? That is the starting point of our journey.

What does love mean to you? It is one of the hardest words to truly understand, most people think it is a vigorous emotion, because it can turn are world upside down for the good or bad. But, it is not an emotion. We sometimes injured the word love when we use it to state our feelings.

I can say, I love chocolate ice cream or my vehicle, this is not love, although I do enjoy a big bowl of chocolate ice cream and have had many vehicles over the years that I have enjoyed driving them, the emotion I am feeling is not love, but pleasure. I am grateful the moments of pleasure.

When we mix emotions and love together, they get jumbled. When we understand our emotions, it is easy to appreciate that love is something else. We can start to use other words for example, I really enjoy a big bowl of chocolate ice cream or I have delight to go to work every day.

Our culture today puts way to much importance on our feelings. We are sometimes told to do whatever makes us feel happy. Emotions and feeling change, it is like the wind here one day and then gone, the next windy day try and catch the wind you can't. Sometime our emotions and feeling are like the winds in a hurricane and sometimes like as a warm breeze.

So if love is not emotion what is it? Genuine love is ever persistent. The reason for that is because we choose to love; that is what is meant by Agape, this is the unconditional love. God has chosen to love us, it is that simple.

We have heard that God is love and John's words tell us, "For God so loved the world that he gave his one and only Son, that whoever believes in him should not perish, but have eternal life. For God didn't send his Son into the world to judge the world, but that the world should be saved through him." John 3:16-17 (WEB).

Let us understand we are here for one reason, only it is not because God needed us and God didn't create the universe and the earth because he had nothing better to do that week. God didn't design us in own image because He was lonely. God chose to create us out of his great love: before anything else was created, God loved us; that is the simple truth. It may be difficult to realize, but, we are loved by God.

When we can grasp the word of God in the Bible, we see this over and over again God's love. He is for us and proved that through Jesus His Son. Yes, Jesus is unique in so many ways, as we go through His statements, we will learn just how unique He really is.

5

The Emphasis of I am

The Emphasis of I am

Jesus made seven I AM statements in the book of John. We already have examined one of the seven. In preparation for the next several messages, let's clarify the phrase "I AM" in reference to the statements that Jesus made about Himself.

Everyone says the phrase "I am". It does not mean that we are professing to be God. We use those words every day without thinking about it. "I am going to work now", "I am their mother or father", "I am the mother of my children from the moment they were born and always will be". We are not claiming we are God. We are simple saying, "I, myself, at this moment and every other current moment, their mother". The term "I AM" is a statement as to what is occurring here and now. That is why in John, Jesus said, "Before Abraham was born, I AM." John 8:58 (NKJV). The people of the day correctly understood what he was saying. Look closely at how Jesus makes this statement. Jesus said before Abraham was born (past tense), and then Jesus jumps to the present (here and now) when He says "I AM."

Jesus clearly is appealing to them the knowledge of the Old Testament and then, using a present tense form of "to be," he says, "I AM." It is a present-tense statement.

The writer of Hebrews makes this very clear when he tells us, "Jesus Christ is the same yesterday, today, and forever" Hebrews 13:8 (NKJV). In this brief statement, God and Jesus are always in the here and now.

So what does the here and now mean to us? It means, the ultimate reality. For a better understanding, let's look at the definition of the word *reality*. The Encarta Dictionary defines it as "actual being or existence, as opposed to an imaginary, idealized, or false nature."

When Jesus makes the statement "I AM," He is telling us that He is the representation of God. Who is Jesus? He is the "I AM." Jesus is equal with God. He is eternal with God. He is everything—at this very moment!

However, how many of us really live in the moment? Our thoughts are often on the past or are on the future. It's natural to spend moments of thought in the past remembering a wonderful events or looking forward to a future event. In our day to day routines, our view is struggles from the past, or becoming restless of the future. Rarely are we fully "in the moment", a state of just being.

Time is a human concept. Time means nothing to God or Jesus. To them, life is the moment. Time doesn't actually exist, it is a balance we use to prearrange our lives to what we label "life". All we have is what we feel right now, the understanding with our five senses, sight, hearing, touch, smell, and taste.

When we allow ourselves to become wounded by time, we are a victim of the past and carry with us a sense of anxiety into the future. We accept this state as a norm in our fast-paced, highly-stressed society. When we live in two worlds the past and the future, we miss the "I AM" moment, to reside in the position of now, enjoying life and happiness.

Take this moment and think about all the wonderful things in your life. Be grateful. Know that at this moment you are one with the creator of this wonderful universe and all that is in it. That God is for you. Don't think about what has happened or what may happen, just relax in the moment.

Mindfulness also involves acceptance, meaning that we pay attention to our thoughts and feelings without judging them—without believing, for instance, that there's a "right" or "wrong" way to think or feel in a given moment. When we practice mindfulness, our thoughts tune into what we're sensing in the present moment rather than rehashing the past or imagining the future. "Look at the birds. They don't plant, harvest, or save food in barns, but your heavenly Father feeds them. Don't you know you are worth much more than they are?" Matthew 6:26 (ERV).

6

I am the Way and the Truth and the Life

I am the way, the truth, and the life

Jesus is eternal with God; He is vital to our immortally. The writer of Hebrews makes this very clear when the author tells us "Jesus Christ is the same yesterday, today, and forever." Hebrews 13:8 (NKJV). In this brief statement, God and Jesus have always been and will always be.

John records this historic account. The book of John is where Jesus made this most noteworthy statement while He was here on earth. Jesus said to John, "I am the way, the truth, and the life. No one comes to the Father except through Me." John 14:6 (NKJV). This specific statement is the most inclusive statement, as Jesus tells us today who He really is and the basis for which He came. These words He expressed confirmed that He indeed was the Messiah.

Let's look at the accurate translation of this statement. This is how it would read in the native Hebrew language translation: "I am the true and living way." So what Jesus really said was, "I am the true way, and I am the living way." It was God's plan from the beginning that mankind would have a way that leads back to a loving and merciful God, for it is only through what Jesus did—by his life, death, burial, and resurrection—that reconciles us to God.

God makes it perfectly clear that this is God's will Salvation is of the Lord. "There is salvation in no one else! God has given no other name under heaven by which we must be saved" Acts 4:12 (NKJV). John makes this even clearer when he writes "For God loved the world so much that He gave His one and only Son, so that everyone who believes in Him will not perish but have eternal life. God sent His Son into the world not to judge the world, but to save the world through Him" John 3:16–17 (NKJV).

So salvation and being reconciled to God is only through life, death, burial, and resurrection of Jesus. It has to be done God's way. We cannot know God by human wisdom or philosophy. This is explained to us in Colossians—"Beware lest anyone rob you through philosophy and vain deceit, according to the tradition of men, according to the elements of the world, and not according to Christ" Colossians 2:8 (NKJV) and again "The world with its wisdom was unable to recognize God in terms of his own wisdom. So God decided to use the nonsense of the Good News we speak to save those who believe" 1 Corinthians 1:21 (GNT).

We need to know God's truth, not merely go through the motions, even though it may be done with sincerity. We all know something that we felt was right, and later we found out that we were wrong. This statement made in Proverbs 14-12 holds all the truth—"There is a way that seems right to a man, but its end is the way of death" Proverbs 14:12 (NKJV).

How reckless are we when we think it doesn't matter what we believe, as long as we are sincere. It does matter. It is a matter of life or death. That is why Jesus made the statement, "I AM the Way."

Some may think that they can earn the right to know God by good works or by saying enough prayers, contributing to charity, fasting, attending religious meetings, lighting candles, or even doing their very best to keep the Ten Commandments. Although these are good, we read: "For by grace you have been saved through faith, and that not of yourselves; it is the gift of God, not of works, lest anyone should boast" Ephesians 2:8–9 (NKJV).

Salvation comes by one way and one way only, and that is God's absolute grace. God has bestowed onto us, through His Son, the honor of being reconciled to Him and His free gift of love and mercy. We could never do enough good works to merit the free and loving gift of salvation.

The life, death, burial, and resurrection of Jesus is the only way. God made it that simple. I think Peter said it best: "Blessed be the God and Father of our Lord Jesus Christ, who according to His abundant mercy has begotten us again to a living hope through the resurrection of Jesus Christ from the dead" 1 Peter 1:3 (KJV).

What does this mean for us today? First let's define the statement:

Way of life—as a particular activity as a way of life for someone, mean<u>s</u> that it has become a very important and regular thing in their life, rather than something they do or experience occasionally.

So does it mean every day we must say certain words? For example, "Sinner's prayer." or doing certain activities. For example reading the Bible or going to church. Our beliefs are not mere words or activities. What Jesus was showing us is a knowing of the Divine Father. Spirituality is really all about how you live, not about what you say or do.

What Jesus is telling us in the book of John, Jesus is talking to God, he asked—"Father, I pray that all who believe in me can be one. You are in me and I am in you. I pray that they can also be one in us. Then the world will believe that you sent me. I have given them the glory that you gave me. I gave them this glory so that they can be one, just as you and I are one. I will be in them, and you will be in me. So they will be completely one. Then the world will know that you sent me and that you loved them just as you loved me." John 17:21-23 (ERV).

Jesus has that oneness with God and he is showing us the way to have it too. Eternal life is the life we have.

Let's look at the second part of this statement, "the truth." What is Jesus saying to us? He is saying that He is the truth. He is not just one who teaches the truth; He is the embodiment of truth. Those who have Christ, have the truth; it is not found anywhere else.

Here is a very *significant* question: do you ever think about the world we live in, not just our streets or towns and cities, but, this big world that God created for us? Do you realize that the one God who created this world sent his Son to pay us an exclusive official visit? God sent His Son as one of us, human, so many centuries ago. Have you ever asked yourself why?

Jesus came to bring to us the message of God's truth. His truth is the only true measure of righteousness and the source of both physical and spiritual realms. Jesus showed us and taught us this while he was physically with us. We need to embrace this truth with much more confidence. This will make us better men and women. When we take hold of this truth, then and only then will we know who is trying to deceive us. This is made clear "See to it, then, that no one enslaves you by means of the worthless deceit of human wisdom, which comes from the teachings handed down by human beings and from the ruling spirits of the universe, and not from Christ. For the full content of divine nature lives in Christ, in his humanity" Colossians 2:8–9 (GNT).

Jesus is the only certainty we have. He fully discloses God's way. He wonderfully qualifies us to be restored to it. Only Christ guides us back to God. His Word tells us this: "Do your best to win full approval in God's sight, as a worker who is not ashamed of his work, one who correctly teaches the message of God's truth" 2 Timothy 2:15 (GNT).

We must embrace the truth. Only here will we find the glorious path to true freedom. Once we understand the truth of His words, we will become changed people.

Just as truth is the very principle of God the backbone of creation, so is Christ. Without Him, one is simply living outside of God's revelation.

We use this word truth as a noun, yet John speaks of truth as a verb, an action. So how do we do truth? We sometimes see truth as a one-sided awareness. We as People believe what we need to believe to maintain our view point as an individual or a group. It is the same when it comes to God. The Pastor said this about God and I don't want to hear anything else. This is very controlling statement. Our thoughts create our entire insight of Life.

God's Word is simple. Brothers and sisters, you are people the

Lord loves. "And we always thank God for you. That's what we should do, because God chose you to be some of the first people to be saved. You are saved by the Spirit making you holy and by your faith in the truth." 2 Thessalonians 2:13 (ERV).

In the Scriptures God says, "Be holy, because I am holy." 1 Peter 1:16 (ERV).

This is a mandate from God the truth. Are we ready to hold to this simple truth and we are HOLY!

Those who don't want to hear the truth will avoid the truth thinking, they have it all figured out. This is what this means, whether or not you want to learn and accept the truth. If we seek, we will find the journey is a progression of new information that make us sensible and stronger each time. Let the words of Jesus motivate to a new life.

So how do we "do" truth? Just like Jesus said "But you must continue to believe this truth and stand firmly in it. Don't drift away from the assurance you received when you heard the Good News. The Good News has been preached all over the world, and I, Paul, have been appointed as God's servant to proclaim it" Colossians 1:23 (NLT).

Do you see the stipulation that Jesus places on us? We are disciples of Jesus if we continue in His Word. By continuing in His Word, we shall know the truth, and it is the truth that shall make us free. Free to enjoy the best that God's has for us. We are delivered, saved, rescued, healed, and made to be in right relationship with God.

Jesus said in "Sanctify them in your truth. Your word is truth." John 17:17 (WEB). God's Word is the truth, and we are made holy through the Word of God. When we know the truth, we are set apart and made holy.

Let us heed Paul's advice as he gave it to Timothy. "A servant of the Lord must not quarrel but must be kind to everyone, be able to teach, and be patient with difficult people. Gently instruct those who oppose the truth. Perhaps God will change those people's hearts, and they will learn the truth. Then they will come to their senses and escape from the devil's trap. For they have been held captive by him to do whatever he wants" 2 Timothy 2:24–26 (NLT).

Now let's look at what Jesus meant when He said, "I am the life." First, let me ask this basic question: what is the origin and nature of human beings? The answer is that you and I are special creations of God, made in His image and likeness. Our special creation gives each an individual worth and value. Because God made us and made us like Him inspirer, you and I are very precious.

God created for us a perfect and beautiful place to inhabit. All God created was acceptable and pleasing. Nothing is lacking, demonstrating how human beings were to exist. With a sudden jolt, the agreement of original creation was torn with discord. Man was "born again" to undo spiritual death; a ferocious discord of shame, anger, jealousy, pride, disobedience, murder, and the accompanying inner heartbreaks, pain, and guilt rushed in and has been carried down though ages.

The Bible endorses that by our nature and carnal minds, we are dead in trespasses and sins; we are unable to walk holy and righteous in our lives. The Word of God says we walk according to the course of this world, according to the prince of the power of the air.

We see this truth as it was inspirer as taught to us impressively in that vision of the prophet Ezekiel, where he was carried out by the Spirit and set down in the midst of an open valley, full of dry bones. "Again he said unto me, Prophesy upon these bones, and say unto them, O ye dry bones, hear the word of the Lord" We are all dead, dry bones, and so we need life restored to us." Ezekiel 37:4 (KJV).

We see death in the sudden level of shame that spread as Adam and Eve acknowledged their nakedness. We see death demonstrated as Adam and Eve evaded God. They had known His love, yet their awareness of guilt caused them to withdraw from Him when they tried to conceal themselves from God's presence.

We see death in Adam's refusal to accept responsibility for

his choice. He tried to transfer the blame, first to Eve and then ultimately to God Himself. We see death on the earth as a result of Adam. We see death in the rage of Cain, whose resentment led him to murder his own brother. We see death in the progression that built up through the generations as mankind reproduced. Lamech broke the configuration of monogamy between a man and a woman in a relationship, which God had ordained. Lamech committed bigamy, and he also cheekily vindicated the murder of another man who had in some way wounded him.

From the above examples, we see that the spirit of invalidation is the central theme to the progression that leads to spiritual death and ultimately, physical death in the world. It was the hook that Satan used in the Garden of Eden to separate mankind from God and from each other. Invalidation and death is displayed each and every time we use the weapon of blame or impose our will on to others within our circle of influence.

Mankind now knows good and evil!

The choice that Adam and Eve made took from us the ability to experience God's best. We have an idea of what the best should be, but only as an idyllic or a wanting plea—a dream. If we can distinguish the meaning of evil far more thoroughly, then we can realize God's best for our lives.

Paul sums this up very clearly. "We know that the Law is spiritual; but I am a mortal, sold as a slave to sin. I do not understand what I do; for I don't do what I would like to do, but instead I do what I hate" Romans 7:14–15 (GNT).

The longer we live, the stronger the realization grows: Paradise is lost.

This is the aftermath of the fall of man and the consequences of the spiritual death that grips humanity. Although this message is sobering, it is brightened by the promise contained in God's unconditional love.

What is that promise? Paul tells us, "And you He made alive, who were dead in trespasses and sins, in which you once walked according to the course of this world, according to the prince of the power of the air, the spirit who now works in the sons of disobedience" Ephesians 2:1–2 (NKJV).

Jesus gave His life for us all of us! Jesus came to restore that life that was lost to us. Jesus came to give us life abundant, and it is available free of cost, because Jesus paid the price for it on the cross.

Jesus told us this: "The thief cometh not, but for to steal, and to kill, and to destroy: I am come that they might have life, and that they might have it more abundantly" John 10:10 (KJV).

So what is Jesus telling us when He said, "I am the way, the truth, and the life"? He was telling us that there is no other way to be restored to life, no other truth, and no other source of life available in this world, other than through the deity of Jesus Christ. He and He alone is the only one who can restore us to the Father and to our lives. He is the only way, truth, and life.

7

The Bread of Life

The Bread of Life

Jesus made another strange but wonderful statement about Himself when He said, "I am the bread of life" John 6:48 (NKJV).

Have you given much thought to bread? Bread is a staple food, a basic dietary element. We could endure for a very long period just by eating bread and drinking water. Bread is such a basic food element. Even the aroma of baking bread can bring wonderful feelings.

Jesus, as always, stated the simple truth. And this is the first of His "I am" statements. Jesus said to them, "I am the bread of life. The one who comes to me will never be hungry, and the one who believes in me will never be thirsty again." John 6:35 (LEB).

Take a moment to think about the meaning of the word *bread* in this verse. The Lord Jesus states that He is the essence of life.

Let's look at the historical account. Jesus had been speaking. The Jewish leaders again were testing Him. They brought up the subject of the manna in the wilderness and challenged Jesus to produce some food. Jesus reminded the Jews that their fathers had eaten the manna in the wilderness, and they were dead.

In other words, manna was for the body only, not the spirit. It did not have any power to give eternal life to those who ate it. We have to understand that bread played a fundamental role in the Jewish people's lives. The Jews were to eat unleavened bread during the Passover feast. They also had a celebration of the exodus from

Egypt. You will recall the account when the Jews were wandering in the desert for forty years. God rained down "bread from heaven" to sustain the nation "Then the LORD said to Moses, Behold, I will rain bread from heaven for you. And the people shall go out and gather a certain quota every day, that I may test them, whether they will walk in My law or not" Exodus 16:4 (NKJV).

We can learn five significant points from this one statement. First, Jesus is the essential of life. Second, the life that Jesus is referring to is not physical life but eternal life. Jesus was trying to tell them (and us today) to stop thinking of the physical realm, change your thinking, and see yourself from the spiritual realm. We are a spiritual being.

The third significant point is in. Jesus answered them, "This is the work of God, that you believe in him whom he has sent." John 6:29 (WEB). Notice the word *believe*. This is an invitation for those who were listening that day (and to us) to believe in Jesus, to believe that He is truly the Son of God. Jesus saw through the Jewish people's pretense. They were pretending that they knew God and were working for God, yet the Son of God stood before them, and they still did not believe. Jesus told them the real work of God is to believe.

Now let's fast forward two thousand-plus years to today. Many people today still seek to earn their way to righteousness by good works. Let me clarify: good works are good, and yes, God tells us to do good works. I am all for that. We should all do good works for God.

What some people do not understand, however, is that good works do not precede salvation. As a believer, each and every one of us should say, "My first and most important good work is I believed in my heart, and I confessed Jesus Christ as Lord." Paul made this clear when he wrote "For with the heart, one believes unto righteousness; and with the mouth confession is made unto salvation. For the Scripture says, "Whoever believes in him will not be disappointed." Romans 10:10 (WEB).

The fourth significant point is that Jesus makes this statement again, but this time he adds to it. "And Jesus said to them, Jesus said to them, "I am the bread of life. Whoever comes to me will not be hungry, and whoever believes in me will never be thirsty." John 6:35 (WEB).

Take note of the words *hunger* and *thirst*. To understand this, we have to look back at another statement that Jesus made during His Sermon on the Mount. "Blessed are those who hunger and thirst after righteousness, for they shall be filled." Matthew 5:6 (WEB).

We should ask, what is *righteousness*? Is righteousness a state of moral perfection required by God from us to have a relationship with Him? Or as we see from history of mankind, we seek to earn our way to righteousness. This is our basic human desire, however if we really want to understand this word we need to look at the biblical times to understand the word righteousness as ancient Hebrews understood the word. The people of that day were nomadic, they traveled a route in a brutal country, staying on a safe course was a matter of life or death as they traveled from pasture to pasture. The simple way to clarify righteous is this he who follows the correct path. So a righteous person is one who follows the path of Jesus.

Furthermore, we are also told that God has placed the hunger for righteousness in our hearts "because what may be known of God is manifest in them, for God has shown it to them. For since the creation of the world His invisible attributes are clearly seen, being understood by the things that are made, even His eternal power and Godhead, so that they are without excuse, because, although they knew God, they did not glorify Him as God, nor were thankful, but became futile in their thoughts, and their foolish hearts were darkened." Romans 1:19–21 (NKJV).

What is Paul saying? Plainly that everywhere we look we see the Creator's beauty, the seas are filled with majestic life, the splendor of nature can bring us to thoughtfulness. Feelings of marvel and awe. The night sky has a radiance that can bring us a sense of harmony, *all is well.*

However in our day to day life, we are too busy to take notice with all to do lists, errands and responsibilities we have, this is why Paul goes on to write, he adds this to his letter from the Psalms of David "What then? Are we better than they? No, in no way. For we previously warned both Jews and Greeks, that they are all under sin. As it is written, 'There is no one righteous; no, not one.' " Romans 3:9-10 (WEB).

We are off the path that God has made for us, trying to make our way, this is the problem that we face every day. We have a desire that we cannot satisfy, a hunger that eats away at us, no matter what we do. This is one of the reasons why Jesus came into the world.

Jesus knows the true path that will fill the hunger in our hearts for righteousness. Jesus did this for us and for the love He has for our Father, through the divine grace Jesus understood the love that our Father has for us and how lost we are.

When Christ lay in the belly of the earth, the divine power of God was shown to the world. You may have thought that the creation of the universe was the utmost demonstration of God's power. Maybe you thought that God parting the Red Sea to deliver His people was the greatest act. But when we truly understand the will of God, we know that these were not God's greatest works. Jesus Christ our Lord's resurrection and ascension required the greatest outflow of divine grace ever known or seen. Paul tells us: "which He worked in Christ when He raised Him from the dead and seated Him at His right hand in the heavenly places." Ephesians 1:20 (NKJV).

The apostle describes the greatest exhibition of divine power. Why? It was because all the hosts of hell and Satan himself were massed together to obstruct God's will. They wanted to keep Christ in the tomb by preventing His ascension. Our God, the God who loves us more then we will ever know, triumphed over every form of opposition. Christ's resurrection and glorification was a shattering defeat of Satan and his hosts and an outstanding manifestation of victorious power.

Jesus did this for all of mankind. When we call Him Lord

and place our faith in Him, our sins are imputed to Jesus, and His righteousness is imputed to us. In Christ is the abundant satisfaction. Only He, Jesus Christ our Lord, can satisfy our hunger and thirst for righteousness, for He is our Bread of Life.

Let us ponder Jesus is the "I AM" the one that stood up for all of us. That is why, my dear brothers and sisters, we call Him Lord—because He is still the "I AM"!

8

I am the Door of My Sheep

I am the door of the sheep

Jesus makes a strange statement "Jesus therefore said to them again, 'Most certainly, I tell you, I am the sheep's door.' "John 10:7 (WEB).

This statement is an amusing verse and can be troublesome for some to grasp. To say that Jesus is a door is weird and wonderful, the word "door" is used over one hundred times within the Bible and has many Spiritual meanings. What an amazing statement that Christ is the Door.

Doors are significant in our lives. They serve a valuable purposes. A door is an entrance or an exit. Doors make our homes, businesses, and cars secure. They safeguard us. When we look at putting a door on our home, we look for a strong door; otherwise, it becomes the weakest point of our home. Doors can be mysterious, what is beyond the door hidden from our sight, a closed door can be full of possibilities, for something wonderful may be on the other side.

To call Jesus a door is a rather odd phrase. What is Jesus telling us? He is saying come in, know me and know my Father, become part of the family. He is the door of opportunity, He is saying, He will keep out the things that would injure us. When we know that Jesus is the door of our lives, then Satan can't do us any harm. Jesus is fully able to safeguard us physically and spiritually.

Let us look again at John 10:9: "I am *the* door: by me if any man enter in, he shall be saved, and shall go in and out, and find pasture"

(KJV). And in John 10:7, "Then said Jesus unto them again, Verily, verily, I say unto you, I am *the* door of the sheep" (KJV).

Notice the word *the*. Jesus is telling us He is exclusive, the one and only; all by Himself that only by knowing him not any other way or anyone else, again He tells them this time adding "So Jesus again said to them, 'Truly, truly, I say to you, I am *the* door of the sheep.' " John 10:7 (ESV); truly, truly reinforces the critical importance of His word.

The door is the entryway into the sheepfold. Let's look at this from an ancient society, especially of sheep and shepherding. Sheep are the only domesticated animal that are the most vulnerable. Sheep graze all day and never look where they are going. This is the main reason they often get lost. Sheep do not have a "homing instinct" as most animals do. Another fact about sheep is, Sheep have tremendous peripheral vision and can see behind themselves without turning their heads. However, they have terrible depth perception. They cannot see what is in front of them. This why if the one sheep steps off an overhang, the others will follow.

A sheep pen was nothing more than a circle of large rocks piled into a wall with a small open space to enter. The sheep at nightfall would be put into the pen to keep them safe. There was no gate or door—just an opening—the shepherd would lay in the opening. He accurately became a door for the sheep. The body of the shepherd kept the predators on the outside and the sheep on the inside.

The number one is significant in the Bible, the significance of this primary number is that it is a symbol of unity. As a fundamental number, it denotes unity; as an ordinal, it denotes primacy. Unity is indivisible (we stand as one); the number is independent of all others, and is the source of all others. And that is why we read, "Neither is there salvation in any other: for there is none other name under heaven given among men, whereby we must be saved." Acts 4:12 (KJV).

What does all this tell us today; Jesus is the door that opens to peace and security. The door for Super-Abundant Life. The word life is the Greek word "zoe" and the verb "to live" to have "zen". It is the essence, the energy, the power of being. This is the life that Jesus wishes for us, it is forever.

What do the words of Jesus teach us? That as believers, we are not like the world around us, and our life is more abundant. We are abundant in agape love. We are more abundant in grace. We are more abundant in hope.

Again Jesus said I AM the door. "If anyone enters through me, he will be saved, and will come in and will go out and will find pasture." John 10:9 (LEB).

Here he is telling us that we will be saved the Greek word *"sozo"* which means we are whole, healed, preserve and well.

Jesus is the only door and that door is open to a super-abundance life.

Paul realized that Jesus is the real door. When we choose to enter in It is a new beginning, we are spotless and in perfect righteousness. Paul said it best "So now there is no condemnation for those who belong to Christ Jesus." Romans 8:1 (NLT).

9

I am the Good Shepherd

I am the Good Shepherd

Here is the fourth of the seven "I AM" statements of Jesus, recorded in John's gospel. After stating that He is "the door" in the book of John, Jesus goes on to say "I am the good shepherd: the good shepherd layeth down his life for the sheep." John 10:11 (RV).

Notice the word the again: The Good Shepherd, meaning Jesus is the only Good Shepherd. Now reflect on the meaning of the word good. It means of high quality, suitable, skilled, virtuous, kind, undamaged, ample, honorable, valid, helpful, genuine, obedient, beneficial and noble. David said it best, he wrote A Psalm of David—"The LORD is my shepherd. I will always have everything I need. He gives me green pastures to lie in. He leads me by calm pools of water. He restores my strength. He leads me on right paths to show that he is good. Even if I walk through a valley as dark as the grave, I will not be afraid of any danger, because you are with me. Your rod and staff comfort me. You prepared a meal for me in front of my enemies. You welcomed me as an honored guest. My cup is full and spilling over. Your goodness and mercy will be with me all my life, and I will live in the LORD'S house a long, long time." Psalms 23:1-6 (ERV).

This is a natural goodness. By using the phrase "the Good Shepherd," Jesus is identifying His inherent goodness, His Love, and His beauty. Jesus alone is the one who pilots, models, safeguards, and develops us for we who are His flock.

To have a better understanding of this image that Jesus was capturing, it is helpful to realize that sheep are powerless. For their well-being, they must be sustained by the keeper of the flock, which is the shepherd. The shepherd must always be attentive to the flock.

In the historic account in the Gospels, we see that Jesus was a Good Shepherd by his approach. He called them by name. Sheep can instantly recognize the voice of a faithful, well-known person. Sheep have exceptional memories. They know their handler. This is why Jesus uses these words: "My sheep hear my voice, and I know them, and they follow me." John 10:27 (RV).

This is one reason the Bible uses sheep and flocks as a relationship between us and Jesus. Just as sheep recognize the voice of the shepherd, we also should recognize Jesus, just as Nathanael did. "Jesus saw Nathanael coming toward Him, and said of him, 'Behold, an Israelite indeed, in whom is no deceit!' Nathanael said to Him, 'How do You know me?' Jesus answered and said to him, 'Before Philip called you, when you were under the fig tree, I saw you.' Nathanael answered and said to Him, 'Rabbi, You are the Son of God! You are the King of Israel!' Jesus answered and said to him, 'Because I said to you, "I saw you under the fig tree," do you believe? You will see greater things than these' " John 1:47–50 (NKJV).

Jesus revealed to Nathanael that He knew him. Nathanael heard His voice and knew Jesus was the Son of God.

We who have believed and have walked through the door, are the body of Christ, the true church. Thus, we are also in the sheep fold. Mortals, yet still the children of God. Unlike the sheep, we face many dangers, deceivers, and oppressors. The Good Shepherd Jesus knows all of us, just as a shepherd knows all his sheep. He safeguards them from all danger, and all his attentions are given to their well-being and provision. Our Shepherd—Jesus does no less, yet so much more. Not only does He care for us, but He has given to us the Holy Spirit that guides us each and every day.

10

I am the True Vine

I am the True Vine

Jesus makes the following statement "I am the true vine and my Father is the gardener." John 15:1 (NIV). What is a vine? It is a plant that supports itself by climbing, twining, or creeping along a surface. Did you ever think about this illustration that Jesus gives us here? He goes on to tell us a story. Let us take a closer look at this to appreciate what Jesus is saying. Jesus is painting a picture using imagery and metaphor, this is why Jesus often used parables or short stories to help the disciples and we understand the truth.

Some refer to this as an allegory or parable given by Jesus, and it is only found in the book of John. Whatever it may be, this historic report presents us with a wonderful picture of the relationship that God and Jesus have. The basic truth appears very clearly—as believers, we are called to have that same relationship. This is where our thinking has to change. It is not about how much doctrinal theology we embrace or what religion we are or the creed we repeat. If we put these things first, it is easy for us to miss the real truth and purpose of our faith.

For us today, in actual fact, we have to know a bit of history; the vine is an icon of ancient Israel. The people of that time would carve it on the temple as a representational to being one with the Vinedresser, God. The twelve tribes of Israel was to be a model to the other nations that were around at that time. The twelve tribes of Israel was supposed display the evidence, of a loving and faithful

God. Let us visualize a grape plant, when the plant is well care for, the vine will produce fruit such as grapes however, if the vine gets broken it will no longer be able to produce fruit.

After Jesus makes this statement He give us more details, "He takes away every branch in me which has no fruit, and every branch which has fruit he makes clean, so that it may have more fruit. You are clean, even now, through the teaching which I have given you. Be in me at all times as I am in you. As the branch is not able to give fruit of itself, if it is not still on the vine, so you are not able to do so if you are not in me. I am the vine, you are the branches: he who is in me at all times as I am in him, gives much fruit, because without me you are able to do nothing. If a man does not keep himself in me, he becomes dead and is cut off like a dry branch; such branches are taken up and put in the fire and burned. If you are in me at all times, and my words are in you, then anything for which you make a request will be done for you." John 15:2-7 (BBE).

It is beneficial to us look closely at His words, what is Jesus telling us? It is easy to understand that God is the Vinedresser, Jesus is the vine and we are the branches. What Jesus said next troubles allot of people "He takes away every branch in me which has no fruit." it sounds like if we are not bearing fruit, God will send us away. This is not what Jesus is saying, for those of us who do not know allot about horticultural it is a normal part of pruning. This practice involves the selective removal of certain parts of a plant; the reason to prune a plants is for the removal, shaping, improving and sustaining health. This is what Jesus goes on to say next, every branch that He prunes is pruned so that it will bear more fruit.

The next words Jesus said was "You are clean, even now, through the teaching which I have given you.", Jesus is telling disciples and us today that it is the understanding of the true word that makes us clean and our relationship with Jesus. Jesus is talking with God "Make them holy by the true word: your word is the true word." John 17:17 (BBE).

Next Jesus said "Be in me at all times as I am in you. As the branch is not able to give fruit of itself, if it is not still on the vine, so you are not able to do so if you are not in me". What does it mean to be in Christ? This statement should not confuse us, basically we live in a house within that house we live in a family, one unit, together.

There an interesting phrase in this next statement Jesus made: "If a man does not keep himself in me, he becomes dead and is cut off like a dry branch; such branches are taken up and put in the fire and burned". What He is saying here, we must always keep the true word of God, we see this over and over in Paul's letters. People would come into a group of believers and twist the true word, when this happens we become severed from Jesus and will cause us to shrink away. Just as sap is essential in maintaining the hydraulic connection between the soil and the atmosphere in a plant. The true work of God is essential for us to grow.

This next statement is wonderful: "If you are in me at all times, and my words are in you, then anything for which you make a request will be done for you."

What magnificent words Jesus is telling us. When we consider how much God loves us and how significant His words are, it becomes incredibly clear to understand what He is telling us. Having a better understanding of a Christ connection, we can embark onto abundant life a free gift given to us from our Father. We realize the hope and we realize that the emptiness is gone. Our lives are now lived out of love, the nature of the Vine is love.

John said it best: "There is no fear in love: true love has no room for fear, because where fear is, there is pain; and he who is not free from fear is not complete in love. We have the power of loving, because he first had love for us." 1 John 4:18-19 (BBE).

11

I am the Resurrection and the Life

I am the Resurrection and the Life

Jesus makes another wonderful statement: "Jesus said unto her, I am the resurrection, and the life: he that believeth on me, though he die, yet shall he live:" John 11:25 (RV).

This is a fascinating historical account; Jesus was sent word that His dear friend Lazarus, the brother of Mary and Martha, had become ill. Learning of Lazarus' illness, Jesus did not immediately leave for Bethany, where Lazarus and his sisters lived. It was two days after receiving the news that Jesus and His disciples traveled to Bethany. Arriving in Bethany, they were given the sorrowful news that Lazarus had been dead for four days.

Martha heard that He was coming, and she ran out to meet Him. Let's consider what was written when Martha and Jesus spoke: "Therefore Martha said to Jesus, 'Lord, if you would have been here, my brother wouldn't have died. Even now I know that, whatever you ask of God, God will give you.' Jesus said to her, 'Your brother will rise again.' Martha said to him, 'I know that he will rise again in the resurrection at the last day.' Jesus said to her, 'I am the resurrection and the life. He who believes in me will still live, even if he dies. Whoever lives and believes in me will never die. Do you believe this?' " John 11:21-26 (WEB).

Jesus had raised two people back to life by the time that Lazarus had died. He raised the widow's son at Nain (Luke 7:11-17) and Jairus' daughter (Luke 8:41-54).

In the Old Testament there are three narratives of people who died and were restored to life. The one that I most appreciate is Elisha. He wanted a double portion of Elijah's spirit. "When they had crossed the Jordan River, after they crossed the river, Elijah said to Elisha, "What do you want me to do for you before God takes me away from you?" Elisha said, "I ask you for a double share of your spirit on me." 2 Kings 2:9 (ERV). Elijah, being under the inspiration of God, then replied that Elisha's request would be granted, provided that the younger prophet was with him at the time he was taken away. We are then told that his request was granted because he had fulfilled that requirement.

When reading 2 Kings the historical account of Elijah remarkable life, we see that he had performed fourteen miracles; it is challenging to think that someone could double that. As we read the historical account of Elisha life, we get to the end of his life he dies with only having done twenty-seven miracles, one short of the double portion. But the story is not over—although you would think it would be, as the man was dead. But as we continue reading the historical account his story is not over we are told about a man's dead body that was thrown into Elisha's tomb. When it fell onto Elisha's bones, it came to life and stood on its feet—the twenty-eighth miracle. Nothing is impossible with God!

Miracles in the Career of Elijah

1. Causing the rain to cease for three and a half years (1 Kings 17:1)
2. Being fed by the ravens (1 Kings 17:4)
3. Miracle of the barrel of meal and cruse of oil (1 Kings 17:14)
4. Resurrection of the widow's son (1 Kings 17:22)
5. Calling of fire from heaven on the altar (1 Kings 18:38)
6. Causing it to rain (1 Kings 18:45)
7. Prophecy that Ahab's sons would all be destroyed (1 Kings 21:22)
8. Prophecy that Jezebel would be eaten by dogs (1 Kings 21:23)

9. Prophecy that Ahaziah would die of his illness (2 Kings 1:4)
10. Calling fire from heaven upon the first fifty soldiers (2 Kings 2:10)
11. Calling fire from heaven upon the second fifty soldiers (2 Kings 2:12)
12. Parting of the Jordan (2 Kings 2:8)
13. Prophecy that Elisha should have a double portion of his spirit (2 Kings 2:10)
14. Being caught up to heaven in a whirlwind (2 Kings 2:11)

Miracles in the Career of Elisha:

1. Parting of the Jordan (2 Kings 2:14)
2. Healing of the waters (2 Kings 2:21)
3. Curse of the she bears (2 Kings 2:24)
4. Filling of the valley with water (2 Kings 3:17)
5. Deception of the Moabites with the valley of blood (2 Kings 3:22)
6. Miracle of the vessels of oil (2 Kings 4:4)
7. Prophecy that the Shunammite woman would have a son (2 Kings 4:16)
8. Resurrection of the Shunammite's son (2 Kings 4:34)
9. Healing of the gourds (2 Kings 4:41)
10. Miracle of the bread (2 Kings 4:43)
11. Healing of Naaman (2 Kings 5:14)
12. Perception of Gehazi's transgression (2 Kings 5:26)
13. Cursing Gehazi with leprosy (2 Kings 5:27)
14. Floating of the ax head (2 Kings 6:6)
15. Prophecy of the Syrian battle plans (2 Kings 6:9)
16. Vision of the chariots (2 Kings 6:17)
17. Smiting the Syrian army with blindness (2 Kings 6:18)
18. Restoring the sight of the Syrian army (2 Kings 6:20)
19. Prophecy of the end of the great famine (2 King 7:1)
20. Prophecy that the scoffing nobleman would see but not partake of, the abundance (2 Kings 7:2)

21. Deception of the Syrians with the sound of chariots (2 Kings 7:6)
22. Prophecy of the seven-year famine (2 Kings 8:1)
23. Prophecy of Benhadad's untimely death (2 Kings 8:10)
24. Prophecy of Hazael's cruelty to Israel (2 Kings 8:12)
25. Prophecy that Jehu would smite the house of Ahab (2 Kings 9:7)
26. Prophecy that Joash would smite the Syrians at Aphek (2 Kings 13:17)
27. Prophecy that Joash would smite Syria thrice but not consume it (2 Kings 13:19)
28. Resurrection of the man touched by his bones (2 Kings 13:21)

The other two historical account that references resurrection are in 1 Kings 17. It is recorded that Elijah raised the widow of Zarephath's son from the dead by calling out to the Lord and then stretching himself across the boy three times. In 2 Kings 4, where we are told that Elisha raised the Shunammite woman's son by lying on him until his body grew warm and then lay on him again. The boy sneezed seven times and opened his eyes—he was alive.

Even in the book of Job; Job makes this wonderful statement when he wrote, "I know that there is someone to defend me and that he lives! And in the end, he will stand here on earth and defend me. After I leave my body and my skin has been destroyed, I know I will still see God. I will see him with my own eyes. I myself, not someone else, will see God. And I cannot tell you how excited that makes me feel!" Job 19:25-27 (ERV).

People all over the world are captivated by the mystery of death, and even more so, wonder about life after death. The French sculptor Rodin endeavored to portray the body and facial emotions of Adam and Eve during their acknowledgment of the first human death, that of their son Abel. The display is not of pain and sorrow but of curiosity about the mystery of death.

Jesus Himself, during the time He was here on earth, restored people to life. Even today, people have testified that they died and then rose again to live. What makes the resurrection of Jesus Christ different and important?

The book of John stands in a class of its own because John's writing has a different style from Matthew, Mark, and Luke. John's writings steer the reader to believe that Jesus Christ is truly the Son of God and to belief in Him. John makes this point ninety-eight times. It is also the only account of Lazarus, which was omitted by Matthew, Mark, and Luke. John is the only book where we read about all seven of the "I AM" statements.

We need to understand the truth of this statement "I AM the resurrection and the life." and why it is different from the other resurrections we have read about in the Bible, as well as why it is important to us today that Jesus said, "I am the resurrection and the life."

Let us take a trip back in time and imagine the scene that took place. Jesus was nearing Bethany. We pick up the events in John 11 "Then Martha, as soon as she heard that Jesus was coming. She went to meet Him, As Martha stood and looked into the face of Jesus, she said, in now Martha said to Jesus, "Lord, if You had been here, my brother would not have died." She goes on to say in "But even now I know that whatever you ask of God, God will give you."

Martha had seen Christ work many miracles. She knew Him and His power could have kept her brother alive. She had hope! She may not have completely understood everything that she had seen and heard, but her belief in her knowledge was strong!

Have you ever pondered on these two words that Martha said "even now"? Martha knew that Lazarus had been in the grave four days. She may have remembered how Christ raised the daughter of Jairus from the dead, but she had just died. She may also have remembered that the son of the widow of Nain had only been dead a short time. Upon this expression of faith, Jesus quickly turned to Martha and said, "Your brother will rise again" John 11:23 (ERV).

Martha's next comment to Jesus was somewhat surprising. She said, "I know that he will rise again in the resurrection at the last day" John 11:24 (ERV). Martha went from the present hope to some date way in the future. Martha presumed Jesus was speaking of the resurrection at the last day. Martha was of Hebrew and had been taught from childhood about the resurrection. She had read the resurrection chapter of the Hebrew Bible in Ezekiel 37. How did Martha go from faith that Lazarus could be risen from the dead in the present to sometime in the future? She really didn't know that Jesus was and is the resurrection and life.

How often do we allow doubt to hinder us from believing who the Lord really is? We presume and allow our own reason to influence our faith (beliefs). That is what Martha had done she knew Jesus but she did not see Him as the resurrection

Jesus' statement that He is the resurrection and the life provides us with an in-depth picture of who Jesus really is. Martha believed that the resurrection was an event. Jesus said that the resurrection is Him. Martha's idea of eternal life was a hypothetical notion; Jesus proved that knowledge of eternal life is a personal relationship. Martha thought victory over death was a future expectation; Jesus corrected her that victory is a present reality.

Martha knew Jesus but did not really know Him. That is why Jesus disputed her knowledge and said, "Do you believe this?" We can understand from her own words she had hope, now Jesus goes on to ask her to have a belief. Jesus pointed out the difference between knowing about Him and knowing Him intimately.

Jesus asked this question because it was time for Martha to test her own faith (belief). It is just as suitable for us today as it was to Martha over two thousand years ago: Do we believe all the promises of God? We know Martha knew Jesus was the son of God the historical tells us that. We too can acknowledge that Jesus is the Son of God, but do we know all the elements that are involved as to who Christ, the Son of God, really is?

Let's now look at what took place at the tomb. Jesus saw her weeping, and the others who came with her were weeping, Jesus groaned in the spirit and was troubled, why was Jesus troubled? The shortest statement in the Bible is "Jesus wept." John 11:35 (RV).

Did you ever ask why Jesus groaned, or why He was troubled

and why He wept? Surely it was not because Lazarus was dead. Jesus knew that Lazarus alive and well. Or perhaps it was because Mary, Martha, and the people were weeping.

One of biggest reasons we fall short in our spiritual growth is: We fail to function as the word of God tells us. Every word that God or Jesus said is ***true***!!!! Most people would say that the Bible is the *True Word of God*. However, what they are really saying is they hear the words and take no action. James tells us "For if anyone is a hearer of the word and not a doer, he is like a man looking at his natural face in a mirror; for he sees himself, and goes away, and immediately forgets what kind of man he was." James 1:23-24 (WEB).

This is why Jesus groaned. They heard all the wonderful words Jesus told them. They saw many wonderful works. But, they did not truly believe.

"Jesus wept." John 11:35 (WEB).

Let us look at why Jesus wept. The shortest verse in the Bible is "Jesus wept." It may be the shortest, but it tells us the most. As we think about those tears that Jesus wept, let us assure ourselves that our God is not willing that any should perish but that all should come to repentance.

We know this because in Peter tells us, "The Lord isn't slow to do what he promised, as some people think. Rather, he is patient for your sake. He doesn't want to destroy anyone but wants all people to have an opportunity to turn to him and change the way they think and act" 2 Peter 3:9 (GWT). This is the meaning of repentance. It is that simple—just change the way we think and act.

This is why Jesus did not race to see Martha and Mary when he first got the news of Lazarus being sick. "Therefore the sisters sent to Him, saying, 'Lord, behold, he whom You love is sick.' When Jesus heard that, He said, 'This sickness is not unto death, but for the glory of God, that the Son of God may be glorified through it.' Now Jesus loved Martha and her sister and Lazarus. So, when He heard that he was sick, He stayed two more days in the place where He was." John 11:3–6 (NKJV).

Was Jesus being slow? No! Was He unconcerned? No! Was He just unmoved by the news? No! What Jesus wanted to know was whether Martha and Mary had changed the way that they thought and acted. At first, it seemed that Martha had changed, but we learned she quickly went back to her old way of thinking. Mary, on the other hand, did not change at all. The people that were with them just fueled their negative belief.

So what is the answer as to why Jesus wept? It was not because Lazarus was dead, nor was because Mary and Martha were miserable and dismal. Jesus wept at how everyone grew feeble, depressed, and unbelieving. All their hope was gone. Jesus wept because He knew they would react the same way when He, their teacher and healer, would be crucified and placed in the grave for three days.

Jesus wept because they still didn't get it. Lazarus' death was evidence of their faith. After all the things that Jesus had said and done, they had learned nothing. They were still self-centered. We know this from the comment the people made around the tomb of Lazarus. "Could not he who opened the eyes of the blind man have kept this man from dying?" The people were challenging Jesus for a miracle. Jesus wept because of the people's unbelief in their own God.

Place yourself at the scene of the tomb. Can you feel the pain, anguish, and despair of those people who loved and lost Lazarus? It is an emotionally charged atmosphere, Jesus feels the explosion of emotions of lost and hurting people. That is why he is groaned. They did not understand that He is the *resurrection* and *life*.

The historic account tells us "Jesus said, 'Take away the stone.' Martha, the sister of him who was dead, said to him, 'Lord, by this time there is a stench, for he has been dead four days.' Jesus said to her, 'Didn't I tell you that if you believed, you would see God's glory?' So they took away the stone from the place where the dead man was lying. Jesus lifted up his eyes, and said, 'Father, I thank you that you listened to me. I know that you always listen to me, but because of the multitude standing around I said this, that they may believe that you sent me.' When he had said this, he cried with a loud voice, 'Lazarus, come out!' " John 11:39-43 (WEB).

How quickly do we put our desires and ambitions into a tomb, roll the rock over them, and say good-bye to our dead dreams inside? Do we truly comprehend the tremendous power and love that God applies in every situation in our lives, or do we weep for ourselves in self-pity? Let's not become like the Jews who mourn at the tomb; or like Mary, who gave up; or like Martha, who just looked at the facts and accepted the death of her brother.

No! Let this account speak to us. Let it allow the light to shine light into our hearts to trust Jesus. Let us believe that Jesus will always come through for us. Let's know without doubt that Jesus wants to remove the stones of unbelief in our hearts. Let's wipe the tears of Jesus and truly follow Him as his disciples.

What did Jesus mean when He said, "I am the resurrection and the life"? Let us pause and consider the meaning of these powerful words. What does the account of the resurrection of Lazarus mean today? It means the same as it did for the disciples and other eyewitnesses in Bethany so many years ago. This occurrence is a demonstration of Jesus' ability to make His resurrection power available to His people today. That means you and me. We know this because in Romans 1:4 (NKJV) states: "Jesus was declared with power to be the Son of God by His resurrection from the dead". Even more than Lazarus' return to physical life, Jesus' own resurrection affirmed that He has all power. Nothing in our lives is beyond His power to transform and to change. Consider this reality.

It is one thing to believe that Jesus has the power to raise us up on the last day. He does, and He will. But it's something else to realize that Jesus' power is unlimited now. We are told, "And be renewed in the spirit of your mind, and that you put on the new man which was created according to God, in true righteousness and holiness." Ephesians 4:23–24 (NKJV).

The Bible tells us "that if you confess with your mouth the Lord Jesus and believe in your heart that God has raised Him from the dead, you will be saved. For with the heart one believes unto righteousness, and with the mouth confession is made unto salvation. For the Scripture says: 'Whoever believes on Him will not be put to shame' " Romans 10:9–11 (NKJV). The words *saved* and *salvation*, in Greek, mean healed, deliver, blessed, health, prospered, made whole, and set apart.

Jesus can bring new life to the deadened areas of our own personalities. Because of Jesus' power, we can risk taking actions that we might otherwise never have the courage to take. We need never draw back from anything God asks, for the unlimited power of new life is ours in Him. Your desires and ambitions did not come from nowhere—they are gifts that God has given you to enjoy and flourish and grow in life. We allow the problems of this world to steal and destroy those gifts. Most important, John give us amazing facts Jesus' power and love for us, shows us an exceedingly excellent picture of God's Son bringing life to people. This is what the new convent means—the Good News!

Jesus has rolled the rock away and called us out of the tomb, removing the grave clothes. We are reconciled! Reflect on this for a moment: "All this is from God, who through Christ reconciled us to himself and gave us the ministry of reconciliation; that is, in Christ, God was reconciling the world to himself, not counting their trespasses against them, and entrusting to us the message of reconciliation." 2 Corinthians 5:18-19 (ESV). This means those of us who truly believe are raised into a new life.

Let us know and believe that Jesus has raised us to a new life with Him. We are made new in Him. May we never forget, the resurrection of Jesus is the most important aspect we can believe! The promise we have in Jesus' resurrection remains forever and has given us a new life now, as well as the kingdom of God, the inheritance, the gift of grace, and everlasting life. In Christ all the promises are yes!

When we understand the promises of Gods we know that he really love us. My dear sisters and brothers in Christ, now you know what Jesus meant when He said, "I AM the Resurrection and the Life." He is still the same today as He was the day He stood at the tomb of Lazarus. Jesus is calling you. Come out of your tomb to a new life! Do you believe?

12

I Am the Light of the World

I AM the Light of the World

In John's gospel, the focus is the Lord's ministry through John's selective use of the number seven, which symbolizes divine completeness. There are seven miracles, seven discourses, and the seven "I AM" declarations within this gospel. The leaders of Israel in that day missed the spiritual point of Jesus' teaching, as do many of us today.

This is the second "I AM" statement that the gospel of John recorded for us; he opens his book with these words Jesus' power "In the beginning was the Word, and the Word was with God, and the Word was God. The same was in the beginning with God. All things were made by him; and without him was not anything made that was made. In him was life; and the life was the light of men. And the light shines in darkness; and the darkness comprehended it not" John 1:1–5 (KJV).

Without light, nothing else matters! So why is light defined in the dictionary as a noun? A noun is a word used to describe a person, animal, place, thing, or abstract idea.

Webster's Dictionary defines "light" as "Something that makes things visible or affords illumination." It defines "dark" as a "place or time of little or no light; in secrecy; in ignorance."

The definition of the word *light* shows us that there is more behind this than meets the eye. We take light for granted every day. Light is essential for life. The sun gives us light to exist here on earth. Without the sun, we would be left in a state of darkness.

Light and dark can never be in the same place at the same time. When we enter our homes or a room at night, the first thing we do is turn on a light, and darkness is gone.

Light and dark or darkness seem to be the main theme throughout the Bible. Light has 272 references, and dark or darkness has 205 references.

Strong's Concordance defines light as "illumination or a physical personality".

Strong's Concordance defines dark as "darkness unhappiness, ignorance, sorrow, and wickedness".

We generally give very little thought to the concepts of light and darkness. The Bible begins the narrative of creation in the first three passages with the words *light* and *darkness*. The first place we see the word *light* in the Bible: "And God said, Let there be light: and there was light" is in Genesis 1:3 (KJV).

We see the word *darkness* in the Bible for the first time in Genesis 1:2 (KJV): "And the earth was without form, and void; and darkness was upon the face of the deep. And the Spirit of God moved upon the face of the waters".

On the first day, God commanded light to shine out of darkness. This is not to be confused with the establishment of the sun, moon, and stars on the fourth day. In 2 Corinthians, Paul draws a parallel between the original separation of light from darkness and the conversion of a sinner:

Paul wrote two letters to the Corinthians we know them as First Corinthians and Second Corinthians, these letters addressed a range of issues that the believers in Corinth were facing. He wrote seeing it is God who said, "Light will shine out of darkness," who has shone in our hearts, to give the light of the knowledge of the glory of God in the face of Jesus Christ. 2 Corinthians 4:6 (WEB).

Paul is referring to the prophecy in Isaiah, when God said "I, God, have called you in righteousness, and will hold your hand, and will keep you, and make you a covenant for the people, as a light for the nations to open the blind eyes, to bring the prisoners out of the dungeon, and those who sit in darkness out of the prison." Isaiah 42:6-7 (WEB).

What is the first thing God commanded? It was light to shine out of the darkness. "He said, 'Let there be light,' and there was light." Genesis 1:3 (WEB). Paul is writing that the same God who formerly commanded light to shine out of the darkness has once again made a way for His light to shine in our hearts and dispel the darkness. Think about how magnificent this is, when we compare it to the beginning of creation.

Our heavenly Father God wanted a family, His very first command was to let the light shine. When God first created mankind, He created us as impeccable beings. The moment that Satan deceived Adam and Eve, all of mankind fell into darkness. God's plans could not be stopped, and that, my dear brothers and sisters, is why the true gospel must be known. The Spirit of the Most High and living God moves on the heart of each and every person, just as He moved on the face of the deep in the original creation.

You can see that God began this world and mankind with light. Likewise, we become a new creation of God in Christ Jesus. God's love shines in our hearts by the Holy Spirit, just like the first creation. Then and only then does our new creation life begin. The old has life passed away, and darkness no longer exists within us anymore.

Paul's life story is a remarkable, thirteen letters in the Bible are credited to him. Paul was a Hebrew from the tribe of Benjamin born in city of Tarsus, grew up in the midst of Greco-Roman and was a Roman citizen. He was an enthusiastic member of the Pharisees. He was highly sophisticated and associated magistrates and philosophers.

On the road to Damascus, Paul learned that the One he had loathed was really the light of new beginnings, and when his sight was restored, he went out to share his illuminated knowledge of the glory of God and the truth of Jesus Christ.

Much of Paul's writing is explaining why God's light shines

in our hearts. As we read in 2 Corinthians 4, one would think this is the purpose of Paul's writings—to give us the light of the knowledge of the glory of God. Although this is true, there is a further depth that we will discover as we explore Jesus' statement, "I am the Light of the world." As you will see, that statement is much more profound.

A considerable part of Paul's writing is focused on explaining why God's light shines in our hearts "Jesus spoke to the people once more and said, 'I am the light of the world. If you follow Me, you won't have to walk in darkness, because you will have the light that leads to life' " John 8:12 (NLT).

Let us see if we can discover what Paul knew about that declaration and what is he trying to teach us.

First, we have to determine what the light of God is *not*. Some people may think that the light of Jesus is a spotlight to point out our faults or sins. The light of God is not aimed at us for interrogation; God knows us better then we know our selves and from His point of view we are forgiven, His word tells us that we are spotless.

This light might be more like a welcoming fire on a cool fall night, where we gather with our friends in the warmth of the flickering flames, drawing us close and comforting us. Or it might be a mood fire, lighting the room on a cold winter night for friendship and intimacy. Could Jesus mean it is like a runway light that gives direction when we get lost? Or could it be just the sun that shines so brightly on a late July afternoon, which keeps us all perfectly warm? Yes, it is all of this and much more.

Let's go back in time and look at another historic account what took place. "On the last day, the climax of the festival, Jesus stood and shouted to the crowds, "Anyone who is thirsty may come to me! Anyone who believes in me may come and drink! For the Scriptures declare, 'Rivers of living water will flow from his heart.' " (When he said "living water," he was speaking of the Spirit, who would be given to everyone believing in him. But the Spirit had not yet been given, because Jesus had not yet entered into his glory.)" John 7:37–39 (NLT).

Notice it said "the last day, the climax of the festival." This was the Feast of Tabernacles. The Feast of Tabernacles, also known as the Feast of Booths, and Sukkot, is the seventh and last feast that the Lord commanded Israel to observe and one of the three feasts that Jews were to observe each year. "Each year every man in Israel must celebrate these three festivals: the Festival of Unleavened Bread, the Festival of Harvest, and the Festival of Shelters. On each of these occasions, all men must appear before the Lord your God at the place He chooses, but they must not appear before the Lord without a gift for Him" Deuteronomy 16:16 (NLT).

The Feast of Tabernacles takes place on the fifteenth of the Hebrew month Tishri. This is the seventh month on the Hebrew calendar and usually occurs in late September to mid-October. The feast begins five days after the Day of Atonement, and at the time, the fall harvest had just been completed. It was a time of joyous celebration as the Israelites celebrated God's continued provision for them in the current harvest and remembered His provision and protection during the forty years in the wilderness.

The Feast of Tabernacles, like all the feasts, was instituted by God as a way of reminding the Israelites in every generation of their deliverance by God from Egypt. Of course, the feasts are also significant in that they foreshadow the work and actions of the coming Messiah. Much of Jesus' public ministry took place in conjunction with the holy feasts set forth by God.

Note: Most scholars would agree that there is a very good possibility that Jesus was born during the time of the Feast of Tabernacles because of what John wrote: "And the Word became flesh and **dwelt** among us, and we beheld His glory, the glory as of the only begotten of the Father, full of grace and truth" John 1:14 (NLT).

John chose some very exclusive words to say that Jesus "dwelt among us." This word *dwelt* simply means to "dwell in a tent/tabernacle."

Most scholars also believe it is very likely that John intentionally used this word to associate the first coming of Christ with the Feast of Tabernacles. Christ came in the flesh to dwell among us, and He is dwelling among us as Lord of Lords today. While we cannot be 100 percent certain that Jesus was born during the Feast of Tabernacles, there is a very strong likelihood that this was the time Jesus was born.

The Gospels record that our Lord Jesus not only celebrated the festival, He also took traditional elements of the celebration and applied them to His own life and mission. We find this particularly in John 7 and 8, where Jesus uses two traditional symbols from the Feast of Tabernacles celebration—water and light—to help the people understand who He is and what He offers.

In order to understand Jesus' teaching here, we need a bit of background from Leviticus 23. There, Moses instructed the people that the first day and the eighth day of the festival were to be special days of rest, set apart from the others. But the seventh day became known as Hoshana Rabba, "the Great Day." The people developed special observances and traditions to mark this special day in Israel. The most spectacular of these was the water-drawing ceremony.

We find God's instructions for celebrating the Feast of Tabernacles in Leviticus 23, given at a point in history right after God had delivered Israel from bondage in Egypt. The feast was to be celebrated each year on "the fifteenth day of this seventh month" and was to run for seven days.

We have looked at a few of John's statements in his book. Let's look at who John was. John was one of the twelve apostles and lived from 6 CE to 100 CE. He was the son of Zebedee and Salome and brother of James. John outlived all the other apostles. He lived a very long life and died a natural death. Also, his mother is believed to have been a sister of Jesus' mother, Mary.

John was the only disciple who was with Jesus Christ from the beginning of his ministry. He was nearby during Jesus' crucifixion and was an eyewitness to Jesus' resurrection. John's writing is unique and different from the other three gospels. The gospels of Matthew, Mark, and Luke are called the "synoptic" gospels. *Synoptic* is a Greek word meaning "having a common view." John's writing reflects something that differs greatly in topic from that of the other three synoptic gospels.

John's gospel excludes significant amounts of information found in the three synoptic gospels, including some surprisingly important episodes: the Sermon on the Mount, the Lord's Prayer, the temptation of Jesus, Jesus' transfiguration, and the institution of the Lord's Supper. John makes no mention of these events. Nor do we read any of the parables in John's writing. What we do find in John's writing is Jesus' early ministry, visits of Jesus to Jerusalem before the Passion Week, the extended farewell discourse, and the resurrection of Lazarus. It is only in John's writing that we find the seven "I AM" statements of Jesus.

As well, John relates the historic account of Nicodemus, explaining the new birth and the Samaritan woman at the well. John's writing is very confident and direct. He is authoritative in his writing. We see this in the way he uses the term "truth." The word *truth* is used more times (forty-six) in the gospel of John than in any other gospel. John describes the incarnate "Word" as "full of grace and truth."

"In the beginning the Word already existed. The Word was with God, and the Word was God. He existed in the beginning with God. God created everything through Him, and nothing was created except through Him. The Word gave life to everything that was created, and His life brought light to everyone. The light shines in the darkness, and the darkness can never extinguish it. God sent a man, John the Baptist, to tell about the light so that everyone might believe because of his testimony. John himself was not the light; he was simply a witness to tell about the light. The One who is the true light, who gives light to everyone, was coming into the world. He came into the very world He created, but the world didn't recognize Him. He came to His own people, and even they rejected Him. But to all who believed Him and accepted Him,

He gave the right to become children of God. They are reborn—not with a physical birth resulting from human passion or plan, but a birth that comes from God. So the Word became human and made His home among us. He was full of unfailing love and faithfulness. And we have seen His glory, the glory of the Father's one and only Son." John 1:1–14 (NLT).

We also read that whereas the Law came through Moses, "grace and truth" came through Jesus. "John testified about Him when He shouted to the crowds, 'This is the One I was talking about when I said, "Someone is coming after me who is far greater than I am, for He existed long before me."' From His abundance we have all received one gracious blessing after another. For the law was given through Moses, but God's unfailing love and faithfulness came through Jesus Christ" John 1:15–17 (NLT).

John also makes mention of "doing the truth," as it relates to coming into the light. "But he who does the truth comes to the light, that his works may be revealed, that they have been done in God." John 3:21 (WEB). This is a peculiar declaration, What John is saying that those who choose have committed their lives to living in love are living their life in the reality of the truth that the word of God tells. They live by faith.

John links "truth" with great familiarity to God and defines a spiritual realm to which we have access. It simply means to have the truth in ourselves. This truth is identical to salvation. When we have a suitable understanding of this, it will produce an appropriate relationship with God. Jesus is truth. His nature and persona convey truth and how salvation is inseparably tied to Him. Jesus also demonstrates the nature of God Himself.

We see this in the Old Testament as part of God's deliverance for the Israelites. It was His provision and protection of them for the forty years they wandered in the wilderness when they were cut off from the Promised Land. "The Lord went ahead of them. He guided them during the day with a pillar of cloud, and He provided light at night with a pillar of fire. This allowed them to travel by day or by night. And the Lord did not remove the pillar of cloud or pillar of fire from its place in front of the people" Exodus 13:21–22 (NLT).

They had visible confirmation of God's presence with them during their time in the wilderness. God's presence, the pillar of cloud and fire, was associated with divine actions. In Jesus' day, the celebration of the Feast of Tabernacles included the lighting of great, golden lamps in the temple court as a reminder of the pillar of fire and cloud. Jesus, as the living Light, challenges people to follow Him, as Israel followed God's earlier light. The same holds true for us today when we understand the truth. God protects us and provides for us as we go through life in the wilderness of this world.

John had a thorough understanding of the Scripture, which is why he chose several themes to intertwine, that Christ is the fulfillment of ancient Israel's sacred celebrations throughout his gospel, such as the Sabbath and the Feasts of Passover and Tabernacles. John saw these sacred observances as an important part of our new covenant. Those events were the shadows of Jesus and His responsibility as our Savior and Redeemer, as John writes in chapters 7 through 9. John was delighted to show his readers what Jesus did and said during the Feast of Tabernacles.

Let's uncover the meaning of Feast of Tabernacles. "You must observe this festival to the Lord for seven days every year. This is a permanent law for you, and it must be observed in the appointed month from generation to generation" Leviticus 23:41 (NLT).

We see that the feast was to be held for seven days. The first day was to be a "holy convocation"; the Hebrew is *"mikra kodesh"*, which means a "holy summons".

At the end of every day around sunset, the lighting ceremony began. This event proved to be the most joyous and festive part of the celebration. In the Court of Women, there were four huge lamps, with four golden bowls at their tops and four golden menorahs (seven-branched lamp stands). This was to commemorate God's leading of their ancestors with the pillar of fire through the wilderness.

A Simple Matter Of Belief

"The Lord went ahead of them. He guided them during the day with a pillar of cloud, and He provided light at night with a pillar of fire. This allowed them to travel by day or by night. And the Lord did not remove the pillar of cloud or pillar of fire from its place in front of the people" Exodus 13:21–22 (NLT).

This spiritual representation was a Light (witness) to the nations. Israel was chosen to be God's light to the world.

"For you are a holy people, who belong to the Lord your God. Of all the people on earth, the Lord your God has chosen you to be His own special treasure. The Lord did not set His heart on you and choose you because you were more numerous than other nations, for you were the smallest of all nations! Rather, it was simply that the Lord loves you, and He was keeping the oath He had sworn to your ancestors. That is why the Lord rescued you with such a strong hand from your slavery and from the oppressive hand of Pharaoh, king of Egypt." Deuteronomy 7:6–8 (NLT).

Simply said, God choose these people to show the world the love of God. God wanted a people whom He could use and work through to show His glory to the world.

The second spiritual presentation was the light that represented the glory of God that once filled the temple where God's presence dwelt in the Holy of Holies. "When the priests came out of the Holy Place, a thick cloud filled the Temple of the Lord. The priests could not continue their service because of the cloud, for the glorious presence of the Lord filled the Temple" 1 Kings 8:10–11 (NLT).

And again "Then the Spirit took me up and brought me into the inner courtyard, and the glory of the Lord filled the Temple" Ezekiel 43:5 (NLT).

There is also a deeper meaning for the four menorahs that were used in the lighting ceremony. Four is often a symbolic number representing geographical completeness, because there are four corners of the world. The four menorahs symbolized the four corners of the world and that the light would be given to everyone who believes in Jesus.

The ceremonial lighting was to symbolize the light of God

being made available to each of us. The Feast of Tabernacles shows us a picture of God's plan. It displayed the pouring out of God's spirit to all and salvation being offered to everyone who calls Jesus "Lord of Lords"!

Water was also an important part of the Feast of Tabernacles. Before the festival, the rabbis would teach on every passage in Scripture dealing with water. During the water-drawing ceremony, the high priest would recite.

"In that day you will sing: 'I will praise You, O Lord! You were angry with me, but not anymore. Now You comfort me. See, God has come to save me. I will trust in Him and not be afraid. The Lord God is my strength and my song; He has given me victory.' With joy you will drink deeply from the fountain of salvation! In that wonderful day you will sing: 'Thank the Lord! Praise His name! Tell the nations what He has done. Let them know how mighty He is! Sing to the Lord, for He has done wonderful things. Make known His praise around the world. Let all the people of Jerusalem shout His praise with joy! For great is the Holy One of Israel who lives among you.'" Isaiah 12:1–6 (NLT).

It was on the last day of the Feast of Tabernacles that the center candle was lit. At the moment of the lighting of the candles, Jesus stood up. "Jesus spoke to the people once more and said, 'I am the light of the world. If you follow Me, you won't have to walk in darkness, because you will have the light that leads to life'" John 8:12 (NLT).

The gospel of John focuses on truths about Jesus, which are essential to our faith. The "I AM" statements that Jesus applies to Himself in the gospel of John are those that draws us to faith, the same as did in the historic account we read in John. "Then many who heard Him say these things believed in Him" John 8:30 (NLT).

These statements, however, promoted anger in some people as the historic account tells us: "At that point they picked up stones to throw at Him. But Jesus was hidden from them and left the Temple" John 8:59 (NLT).

Texts such as this one do not leave us with a feeling of love and warm-heartedness; rather, they leave us somewhat troubled.

It is the same today as it was in the day of John. There are ridiculers and doubters. Some people may ask why the "I am" statements were left out of Matthew, Mark, and Luke. Why couldn't Matthew, Mark, Luke, and John agree that they were important?

The four gospels were written solely to summarize the historical account of the life of Jesus. Each gospel is aimed at a certain group of people. The outlines are represented in a way that is profound to each group of people.

The gospel of Matthew was written to the Jewish people. The purpose was to establish proof by presenting that Jesus was Israel's long-awaited Messiah. Matthew begins his gospel with genealogy: "This is a record of the ancestors of Jesus the Messiah, a descendant of David and of Abraham" Matthew 1:1 (NLT).

Throughout the gospel, Matthew chooses these words: "it was fulfilled." Another important fact is that the first miracle Matthew records is the cleansing of a leper. Today, this means very little, but to the Jewish people of Matthew's time, it had great meaning. Leprosy was regarded as a punishment for sin. When Jesus cleansed the leper, it demonstrated to the Jewish people the taking away of the sin of their nation.

The gospel of Mark was written to the Romans. The purpose of this gospel was to portray Jesus as the obedient servant of God and the Good News about Jesus, the Son of God. "The beginning of the gospel of Jesus Christ, the Son of God" Mark 1:1 (NKJV).

Mark begins with the public ministry of Jesus. The gospel of Mark is sometimes called the "snapshot" gospel, because it gives us a play-by-play photo shoot of Jesus' activity. The first miracle we read is the casting out of a demon. The reason for this is that the Romans worshipped many gods. This act established to the Romans that God, who sent Jesus and who Jesus served, was the Most High God and above all other gods. This was of great importance to the Rome's polytheistic society.

The gospel of Luke was written to the Greeks. Luke opens his gospel with these words: "Inasmuch as many have taken in hand to set in order a narrative of those things which have been fulfilled among us." Luke 1:1 (NKJV).

The Greeks were famous for their storytelling form of debating. This is why Luke frequently chooses these words: "and it came to pass." Luke's writing bestows Jesus' human side and stresses Jesus' teachings. The gospel represents Jesus as the Son of Man, as Jesus often referred to Himself. To make his case, Luke outlines Jesus' genealogy from Adam to Jesus, as Adam was the first man. The Greeks, much like the Romans, were a polytheistic society. Luke also chose to use the casting out of the same demon as Mark used as his first miracle.

An interesting fact: When movies are made for TV or the big screen about the life of Jesus, it is the gospel of Luke that is most often used, as it is written in narrative form.

This brings us back to the gospel of John. John wrote to the body of Christ (the church)—this is an exclusive gospel. John opens his gospel before time and identifies Jesus as the Eternal One who was with God and who was God. "In the beginning was the Word, and the Word was with God, and the Word was God." John 1:1 (NKJV).

The first miracle John records was the changing of water into wine. That account is a life-changing moment symbolically to His disciples. "This beginning of signs Jesus did in Cana of Galilee, and manifested His glory; and His disciples believed in Him" John 2:11 (NKJV).

Changing water into wine was a sign. It was a phenomenal act with a spiritual meaning. It shows that Jesus was undeniably the Son of God. Jesus demonstrated the power of God. Wine symbolized the joy of life, which is what Jesus brings to the world.

John's gospel is also very interesting with regard to the period of time it includes. John only records a fraction of Jesus' three-and-a-half-year ministry. Almost half of the gospel of John covers just one week within the three and a half years, and some of the verses are noted as just a day. John wrote what was most important to the body of Christ (the Church) believers: the seven discourses, seven miracles, and the seven "I AM" statements.

There is another mystery: the first chapter of Ezekiel tells us of a historic account where the glory of God was among the captives. Ezekiel had a vision. He saw a violent whirlwind coming from the north. He also saw four living creatures, each of which had four faces—lion, ox, eagle, and man. This vision was Ezekiel's call to the prophetic ministry.

Another mystery is the account in Exodus. After the children of Israel left Egypt, they were instructed to set up in four sub-camps. The tabernacle was in the center of the camp. The first camp was to the east and was called the camp of Judah. They had a flag with a large lion stitched on it. The second camp was called Ephraim and was positioned opposite in the west. On that flag was stitched the diagram of an ox. The third camp was positioned to the south. That flag had a face of a man stitched on it. The fourth camp was positioned to the north. That flag had a diagram of a large eagle stitched on it.

These four flags signify the four gospels: the gospel of Matthew is the lion (the lion of Judah); the gospel of Mark is the ox, being a beast of service; the gospel of Luke is the man (the Son of Man); and the gospel of John is the eagle, a symbol of royalty, because of Jesus. "But you are a chosen generation, a royal priesthood, a holy nation, His own special people, that you may proclaim the praises of Him who called you out of darkness into His marvelous light." 1 Peter 2:9 (NKJV).

When we truly understand the meaning of the four gospels, we see the four faces of Jesus. We can begin to see what God sees when He looks at us in Christ. The four points of the world—north, south, east and west—in the form of a cross, with God at the center, are one nation brought together by the love of God through His Son, Jesus.

Now we have a greater historic clarification and better understanding of the four gospels and the Feast of Tabernacles when Jesus makes the statement "I am the light of the world" in John's gospel.

We should also have a better understanding of the pouring of the water and the lighting of the candles and how important that ritual was on the last night. As they lit the candles, they remembered that during the day, the children of Israel were led by a light that was in a form of a cloud, and at night, they were led by a pillar of fire, a flaming light in the darkness of the night. The Feast of Tabernacles was to honor the light that led the children of Israel. As we saw, it was at the moment when they lit candles on the final day of the ceremony that Jesus made that statement.

If this is all the information we have to go by, it makes Jesus' statement remarkable. Let's identify **this word, *light*. The first place we see the word *light* in the Bible is the very first words from God.** "In the beginning God created the heavens and the earth. The earth was without form, and void; and darkness was on the face of the deep. And the Spirit of God was hovering over the face of the waters. Then God said, '*Let there be light*'; and there was light. And God saw the light, that it was good; and God divided the light from the darkness." Genesis 1:1–4 (NKJV).

We see this again in Isaiah: "I, the Lord, have called You in righteousness, And will hold Your hand; I will keep You and give You as a covenant to the people, As a light to the Gentiles, To open blind eyes, To bring out prisoners from the prison, Those who sit in darkness from the prison house." Isaiah 42:6–7 (NKJV). In Isaiah 49:6 (NKJV), we read : "Indeed He says, 'It is too small a thing that You should be My Servant To raise up the tribes of Jacob, and to restore the preserved ones of Israel; I will also give You as a light to the Gentiles, That You should be My salvation to the ends of the earth' ".

Do you understand what Jesus was saying when He said "I am the light of the world"? He is Israel's long-awaited Messiah. The children of Israel knew that God was going to send a light to the nations.

We can draw even more insight about this from reading

Malachi: " 'For behold, the day is coming, Burning like an oven, And all the proud, yes, all who do wickedly will be stubble. And the day which is coming shall burn them up,' Says the Lord of hosts, 'That will leave them neither root nor branch. But to you who fear My name The Sun of Righteousness shall arise With healing in His wings; And you shall go out And grow fat like stall-fed calves. You shall trample the wicked, For they shall be ashes under the soles of your feet On the day that I do this,' Says the LORD of hosts." Malachi 4:1–3 (NKJV).

Did you notice what God is saying? In the phrase "the Sun of Righteousness," the word sun is not the noun, son.

Jesus gives us more insight: "I tell you the truth; this judgment will fall on this very generation. 'O Jerusalem, Jerusalem, the city that kills the prophets and stones God's messengers! How often I have wanted to gather your children together as a hen protects her chicks beneath her wings, but you wouldn't let Me. And now, look, your house is abandoned and desolate. For I tell you this, you will never see Me again until you say, 'Blessings on the One who comes in the name of the Lord!' " Matthew 23:36–39 (NLT).

There is a story that depicts this scripture so beautifully: One day a farmer had a devastating fire that burned everything—nothing was left. As the farmer walked around the farm after the fire was extinguished, he noticed a carcass of a chicken that was almost indistinguishable, with its wings spread out fully. The farmer lifted up the carcass with his boot and kicked it aside. As he did that, several chicks scurried out from under the carcass. That is a picture of what Jesus did for us on the cross. He took the scorching fires of hell upon Himself so that we would be saved.

"Coming to Him as to a living stone, rejected indeed by men, but chosen by God and precious, you also, as living stones, are being built up a spiritual house, a holy priesthood, to offer up spiritual sacrifices acceptable to God through Jesus Christ. Therefore it is also contained in the Scripture, "Behold, I lay in Zion a chief cornerstone, elect, precious, and he who believes on Him will by no means be put to shame." Therefore, to you who believe, He is precious; but to those who are disobedient, "The stone which the builders rejected has become the chief cornerstone," and "a stone of stumbling and a rock of offense." They stumble, being disobedient to the word, to which they also were appointed." 1 Peter 2:4–8 (NKJV).

They knew that God was the essence of light, and the Messiah from God would also be light. This is why John chose these words: "God created everything through Him, and nothing was created except through Him. The Word gave life to everything that was created, and His life brought light to everyone. The light shines in the darkness, and the darkness can never extinguish it." John 1:3–5 (NLT).

"He was the true Light; He enlightens every man coming into the world." John 1:9 (LITV).

Jesus came as the Light that the messianic prophecies said God would send. Expanding on this statement: "Then Jesus again spoke to them, saying, I am the Light of the world. The one following Me will in no way walk in the darkness, but will have the light of life." John 8:12 (LITV).

Light is an entity. Jesus is the Light that the children of Israel followed around for years in the wilderness. It moved every day and night for forty years. Jesus is saying, I am that light; follow Me. What does it mean to follow Jesus? If you really desire to follow Jesus, He has to become everything to you, and you believe all He has told you. We all follow or believe something, such as our friends, our family, culture, or our own selfish desires. Jesus tell us, "No one is able to serve two lords; for either he will hate the one, and he will love the other; or he will cleave to the one, and he will despise the other. You are not able to serve God and wealth." Matthew 6:24 (LITV).

When we choose to follow Jesus, it means we strive to be like Him. We make Jesus Lord of our lives. We do this by every choice we make that has been refined through His words. Our only objective should be to glorify God through His Son, Jesus. **"Then**

whether you eat or drink, or whatever you do, do all things to the glory of God." 1 Corinthians 10:31 (LITV).

We choose to follow Jesus simply because we want to. Thus, we have "I am life." When we choose to believe, a divine Light floods our dead spirit being and regenerates us to a new living spirit. The divine Light streams into our living spirit and opens the eyes of our hearts, giving us eternal sight. This divine Light is the same light that God has used to make everything in our world good. Then and only then can we live a life that God has planned from the beginning for us.

We can live our life in the light of Jesus Christ, knowing that in Him, we will never walk in darkness. By walking in His light, Christ can be reflected through us, and we become a light for others. And since we now know that the gospel of John was written to us who believe and follow Jesus, let his word bring forth the Light that gives life. **"In Him was life, and the life was the light of men."** John 1:4 (NKJV).

Father, I give the glory to You. With what we have learned
about Jesus, the divine Light of the
world, I pray that we will all continue to grow,
to cherish Your Son, each and every moment of every day.

And Father, we thank You for making us the children
of the Light. We walk as children of the Light
and live the life that brings glory to You.

Amen...

Conclusion

We can all agree and believe that Jesus Christ is the Son of God and that He died on the cross for our sins, yet this is not enough, because even Satan has that belief. Do you find this shocking? James tells us, "You believe that there is one God. You do well. Even the demons believe—and tremble! But do you want to know, O foolish man, that faith without works is dead?" James 2:19–20 (NKJV).

"You were the anointed cherub who covers; I established you; You were on the holy mountain of God; You walked back and forth in the midst of fiery stones. You were perfect in your ways from the day you were created, Till iniquity was found in you. By the abundance of your trading you became filled with violence within, And you sinned; Therefore I cast you as a profane thing Out of the mountain of God; And I destroyed you, O covering cherub, From the midst of the fiery stones." Ezekiel 28:14–16 (NKJV).

Satan knows the truth better than most people today do. He believes and knows that there is one God and that Jesus is the Lord of the world. But does his "belief" save him?

We receive Jesus Christ by faith, and faith is what we believe. As an act of our will and what we choose, the thoughts of our minds become what we believe, and what we believe becomes our opinion. We are, then, the sum total of what we believe.

Paul also tells us: "For those who live according to the flesh set their minds on the things of the flesh, but those who live according to the Spirit, the things of the Spirit." Romans 8:5 (NKJV). So, if we believe according to God's beliefs, then there is no limitation on God's grace in our lives.

So who is Jesus Christ to you? Is Jesus the living image of God to you?

He is the reflection of God's glory and the exact likeness of his being, and he holds everything together by his powerful word. After he had provided a cleansing from sins, he sat down at the right hand of the Highest Majesty and is much superior to the angels as the name he has inherited is better than theirs. For to which of the angels did God ever say, "You are my Son. Today I have become your Father"? Or again, "I will be his Father, and he will be my Son"? And again, when he brings his firstborn into the world, he says, "Let all God's angels worship him." Hebrews 1:3–6 (ISV).

"The god of this world has blinded the minds of those who don't believe. As a result, they don't see the light of the Good News about Christ's glory. It is Christ who is God's image." 2 Corinthians 4:4 (GWT).

What does it mean to know someone? Think of all the people you are acquainted with, how well do you know them? When Jesus said He knows the Father, this means that He has complete trust, no skepticism; there is harmony in that kind of believed it is the vital link to the union of life. That is what Jesus hopes we will understand. It is not difficult to identify that Christ is in the believer, and the believer is in Christ at the same time.

You may have read or heard the usual illustration of a poker in the fire. Not only is the poker in the fire, but the fire is in the poker. This is a feeble illustration, the poker is only reacting to the fire. A better illustration would be a military marching band, each one of the band members knows the other and together they become one unit. Another illustration that could simplify the meaning is the Blue Angels precision flying. Both these illustrations show us one unit.

Jesus asked this of God: "Not for these only do I pray, but for those also who will believe in me through their word, that they may all be one; even as you, Father, are in me, and I in you, that they also may be one in us; that the world may believe that you sent me." John 17:20-21 (WEB).

Jesus is talking about oneness, it is our connection to Jesus and the understanding of the word of God that brings us into that oneness. God is not in some far off place, where we and Jesus are there too.

Jesus tells us "On that day you will know that I am in my Father and that you are in me and that I am in you. Whoever knows and obeys my commandments is the person who loves me. Those who love me will have my Father's love, and I, too, will love them and show myself to them." John 14:20–21 (GWT).

What day is Jesus referring to? The day we know Him as He is that we are in union with Him. Then he said obey my commandments. What are his commandments? Love God, Love ourselves and our neighbors and that we will know the nature and fulfillment of in Christ. Jesus came to save us, He has made us whole, healed us, preserve us and all is well. We now are at peace with God! No matter what, God is still madly in love with us.

"For God did not send His Son into the world that He might judge the world, but that the world might be saved through Him. The one believing into Him is not condemned; but the one not believing has already been condemned, for he has not believed into the name of the only begotten Son of God." John 3:17–18 (LITV).

"Then being justified by faith, we have peace with God through our Lord Jesus Christ, through whom also we have had access by faith into this grace in which we stand, and we glory on the hope of the glory of God." Romans 5:1–2 (LITV).

When we truly look at the word of God and understand what Jesus is telling us, can we have faith beyond doubt? Paul said this: "There is therefore now no condemnation to those in Christ Jesus, who do not walk according to flesh, but according to Spirit. For the Law of the Spirit of life in Christ Jesus set me free from the law of sin and of death." Romans 8:1–2 (LITV).

It starts with a simple belief and grows into real faith. This happens when we put our faith in God's Word, The mistake that we most often make is placing our faith in the doctrines. We believe the doctrines, and that is why we see little to no change in our lives. We fail to connect with the true Word.

That is what Paul was doing once he had connected with the living Word of God, he realize it was not about doctrines; It is about love and that is what he wrote to the Ephesians: "For by grace you have been saved through faith, and that not of yourselves; it is the gift of God, not of works, lest anyone should boast. For we are His workmanship, created in Christ Jesus for good works, which God prepared beforehand that we should walk in them." Ephesians 2:8–10 (NKJV).

In Genesis the Word of God tells us that he created us in His own image. He created us just like Himself. He didn't make us mindless androids. He made us in His own likeness and gave us freedom of choice.

John was fisherman by trade before Jesus called him to join him. During that time he got to know Jesus; John wrote down his knowledge and the historic events that took place to reveal that information to a wide-range of people of his day and to us today. John starts by declaring that Jesus knew God from the beginning, emphasizing on Jesus' exceptional relationship with God the Father. The metaphors that Jesus expressed, was to help us understand His relationship toward us and with the Father.

John tell us that we gain spiritual insight and wisdom, he gives details that Jesus has given us unlimited access to the Kingdom of God. He also tells us that we eternal beings and will be with God forever; our gratitude and love are the most important thoughts and feelings we can have for each other.

When God created us, He didn't make us mindless automatons. He made us in His own likeness and gave us freedom of choice. What do you choose to believe? Life is full of choices, when we obtain new information it is difficult to change our beliefs, it is not that simple. We can't influence our minds to believe the information we feel is wrong.

Finally, why should we believe in Jesus Christ? Religion will not become a power in anyone's life, as long as we think of it as something impersonal. The reason for much of the present-day lack of faith on the part of professing Christians, the reason for so much selfishness today and broken marriages and troubled homes, lost hopes, and immorality, is because Christ, to most people, is a myth, a mystery, and a figure of the past, not a living, guiding, empowering, saving Person. We don't have a belief in merely a historic person who lived on the earth some two thousand years ago. Jesus certainly is not dead. He is very much alive, and He is the same yesterday, today, and forever! Both He and God are still madly in love with us.

The prophets of old gave us truth for the future. Jesus came and told us many other truths. When we put all this information together, it is all very clear. The best-known verse in the Bible states the whole story:

"For God so loved the world that He gave His only begotten Son, that everyone believing into Him should not perish, but have everlasting life." John 3:16 (LITV).

God loves all of us, His Son restored us all to Him. If we choose to believe the truth, it is not hard to understand. It is just a **simple matter of belief**.

Bibliography

Strong, James, The Exhaustive Concordance of the Bible, Cincinnati: Jennings & Graham Copyright 1981

Merriam-Webster.com. 2011. https://www.merriam-webster.com (8 May 2011)

Encarta Dictionary

Green's Literal Translation (LITV). Scripture quoted by permission. Copyright 1993 by Jay P. Green Sr. All

Lexham English Bible, (LEB)

The New Living Translation (NLT)

American Standard Version (1901) (ASV)

Bible in Basic English (BBE)

English Standard version (ESV)

New King James Version (NKJV)

The Living Bible (TLB)

World English Bible

East To Read Version (ERV)

King James Version (KJV)

Good News Translation (GNT)

Revised Version (RV)

God's Word Translation (GWT)

New Living Translation (NLT)

About the Author

A miraculous encounter happen to Sharon White about eighteen years ago that changed her whole life. She set out on a journey to find the Truth and to seek a deeper reality; her passion and commitment over the years has given her great insight into the love that God has for each and every one of us.

Before her encounter, Sharon lived in Montreal, QC, Canada and worked as accountant. In her twenties, as single parent with two children, she moved from Montreal to Alberta in order to provide a better home for her family. Sharon drove long haul trucking across Canada and the United States. As her children got older, she started her own accounting business.

Throughout her life, Sharon had many difficulties; from brutal depression to alcoholism. Today, Rev. Sharon White is a confident, successful, spirit filled women; now a grandmother of three wonderful grandchildren, joyfully married to Neil, operates two flourishing businesses and has a fruitful ministry in Alberta, Canada.

In addition, her main passion is serving people. Sharon's weekly commitment to teaching has aided others in finding the Truth in the Word of God; helping others to establish and grow in a relationship with God through the understanding of the life of Jesus Christ and his relationship with the Father and us.

About the Book

There is a difference between knowledge and belief. Knowledge is necessary in our lives. Without knowledge there would be allot of things we could not do. However, belief is likewise significant. An example of this is when we see dark clouds in the atmosphere we know it is going to rain, so our belief is dark clouds mean it will rain. When we base your belief on truths, beliefs will become firm. This is why our beliefs are influenced by the knowledge we have.

When we say we have a belief in the Creator of the universe; what is our knowledge of that belief? Gathering together weekly or reading texts as a group? No, it is getting to know Jesus Christ personally and experience His character. Religious beliefs are a substitute, with ceremony and rituals, for a genuine relationship with God. The knowledge we must seek is true value of the Word of God.

Jesus Christ is the fulfillment of that Word and our spirituality. Jesus is the One to who we need to join with. If you are truly interested in discovering the true Knowledge of Creator of the universe, join me on the journey through a Simple Matter of Belief.